THE PANDEMIC INFORMATION SOLUTION

Overcoming the Brutal Economics of Covid-19

THE PANDEMIC INFORMATION SOLUTION

*Overcoming the Brutal
Economics of Covid-19*

JOSHUA GANS

ENDEAVOR
LITERARY PRESS

Table of Contents

Preface

My Covid-19 pandemic story is that I wrote a book on the pandemic. Actually, two books, a couple of papers, lots of opinion pieces, and a newsletter. All about the pandemic. And now I have written another book.

This one is a sequel to *The Pandemic Information Gap: The Brutal Economics of COVID-19*, which was published by MIT Press in November 2020. I finished that book in July, but by December, I realized that there was more to say. *The Pandemic Information Gap* set up the issue, but it offered little in the way of details. During months of study, I discovered that the details mattered. While working on an initiative to bring rapid antigen screens to workplaces at scale, I also found that these crucial details were often misunderstood by people, including policymakers. As a translator of economic thinking for this crisis, I saw the need to bring more clarity by writing this book.

Why a book? Since August 2020, I have been writing a newsletter every other day about how Covid-19 issues intersect with economics in the context of daily events.[1] This book aims to unify and clarify some larger themes. In addition, we now have real solutions to the information problems that pervade today's pandemic management. Therefore, I saw an important need to present these solutions in one manuscript.

---

[1] The newsletter can be read at https://joshuagans.substack.com.

Who is this book for? My previous Covid-19 book had a wide audience in mind. This time, my audience comprises people who are dealing with the day-to-day challenge of sustaining economic activity while the pandemic rages. What I offer here are solutions, along with the arguments that support them. The book will be of use to people looking for those solutions, including policymakers.

The pandemic creates an urgent need for solutions. I have been writing about the pandemic for almost a year and I know how quickly things can change. Some issues become more (or less) important and salient. So, I plan to update this book and produce new editions as needed. It will evolve while I also keep readers up to date through my newsletter.

As with my previous book on this topic, I could not have written this one without help. I am grateful to Carl Bergstrom, Thomas Hellmann, Richard Holden, Andrew Leigh, Deb MacKenzie, Tiff Macklem, Lukasz Rachel, and Alex Tabarrok. They all, at different times, have helped me think through the arguments presented in this book. Thanks also to Glenn McMahan for copy editing this book in record time. I also owe a special debt to my frontline, rapid screening colleagues: Ajay Agrawal, Chris Deverell, Avi Goldfarb, Chuck Lamarre, Laura Rosella, Sonia Sennik, and Janice Stein. They inspired me to keep going and fighting for these solutions. Each is a world-leading driving force in the effort to get these solutions into the field. I hope that a future edition of this book can describe in detail what the group[2] has achieved.

Joshua Gans
January 2021

---

[2] Creative Destruction Lab Rapid Screening Consortium, https://www. cdlrapidscreeningconsortium.com.

"Solve the pandemic information problem, save the world."
The Pandemic Information Gap

1
The Gap

Pandemics are known to be public health crises. Spreading viruses can have widespread, serious, and even fatal health consequences. To counter them, people need to be protected, treated and, eventually, vaccinated.

Pandemics also have dire economic consequences. The health-care costs are significant, but in many respects, they pale in comparison to the economic and social costs that occur as people seek to protect their health. Some health protections—mandatory distancing, lockdowns, travel restrictions, personal protective equipment, and mask wearing—are imposed by governments. Covid-19 has demonstrated that people will protect themselves even without government mandates.

Efforts to protect health during this pandemic have resulted in major disruptions. Workers have abandoned city centers and chosen to work from home. Leisure activities—travel, going out, hanging out—have been shunned. As schools have closed, it has been hard, if not impossible, for parents (especially women) to work. This has resulted in some of the largest additions to unemployment queues in history and a long-lasting recession. Governments have tried to stem the economic consequences with rent and mortgage protections, handouts, business loans, and the like, but nothing has shielded people from the life-changing consequences of the

Covid-19 pandemic. And, in contrast with previous recessions, this time the less well-off have suffered most.[3]

These economic consequences are caused by the public health crisis; therefore, a full resolution of that crisis would resolve them. But the scale of this crisis is such that its resolution will take time.

The fundamental problem we face in the meantime is an information problem. Specifically:

The economic costs of the pandemic arise from the fundamental problem that we cannot tell who is infectious in order to isolate them from others.

I described this conclusion in *The Pandemic Information Gap*. If we had a way to quickly determine who is infectious, we could separate them from others and protect people as they go about their business. The problem we have faced with Covid-19 is that this information gap has been wide. In July 2020, for instance, a study from England showed that, at that time, only one in 3,900 people were infectious with Covid-19.[4] However, because we did not know the identity of that one infectious person, 3,899 other people treated each other as infectious. When you believe most people could be infectious, you stay away from all people.

The logic behind this conclusion is simple. Pandemics are a problem because the disease spreads from infectious people to susceptible people. As a result, we deal with pandemics solely with health measures, such as developing a vaccine or by isolating people. These options are either slow or very costly.

By contrast, what might happen if we could manage pandemics as an information problem? In this case, we would

---

[3] Titan M. Alon, Matthias Doepke, Jane Olmstead-Rumsey, and Michele Tertilt, "The impact of Covid-19 on Gender Equality," (Working Paper, No.26947, NBER, 2020).

[4] Office for National Statistics (UK), https://www.ons.gov.uk/peoplepopulationandcommunity/healthandsocialcare/conditionsanddiseases/bulletins/coronaviruscovid19infectionsurveypilot/england9july2020.

focus on identifying infectious people and isolating only those individuals. To accomplish this, we would need a method of identifying infectious people.

For some pandemics, the nature of the disease solves the information problem for us. With some viruses, people show symptoms when they are infected. This is what happened during the SARS, MERS, and Ebola outbreaks. Consequently, those pandemics could be suppressed in a matter of months.

Unfortunately, Covid-19 spreads even when people are asymptomatic. Taking this into account, some countries (e.g., Taiwan, Iceland, Mongolia, and South Korea) treated Covid-19 as an information problem from the start. They quickly developed tests and used them to test broad sections of the population. Then they used contact tracing to identify who was more likely to be infectious. By treating the spread of Covid-19 as an information problem, these countries were able to turn their pandemics into something relatively short-lived, like a SARS outbreak.

None of this is news, but many countries still have not taken seriously the idea that stemming the spread of Covid-19 requires solving the information problem. Some countries are doing a good job of using better tests and of implementing a test, trace, and isolate regime. And those efforts have helped to suppress outbreaks and to avoid larger lockdowns. Nevertheless, the outcomes would be much better if every nation did more to solve the information gap.

It is true that outbreaks have emerged following the suppression of the virus in countries that have treated the pandemic with information-based measures, such as in Australia and New Zealand. But those outbreaks did not occur because the information problem was treated lightly; rather, the outbreaks happened due to leaks in the "isolate" action that needs to be enforced. Covid-19 is a sly beast that can quickly run rampant when a population is going about business as usual. There will be no perfect solution, but evidence suggests that countries can avoid the costs associated with Covid-19 by prioritizing solutions to the information problem.

Solutions to the Information Problem

The Pandemic Information Gap set up the problem. This book is a guide into the solution. Much of the book is devoted to describing how the problem can be solved by directly setting up a testing or screening regime that can operate at scale. This approach would enable us to avoid all of the costs associated with managing Covid-19 solely as a health problem. In a blog post, economist John Cochrane neatly summarized this view:

> A vaccine is a technological device that, combined with an effective policy and public-health bureaucracy for its distribution, allows us to stop the spread of a virus. But we have such a thing already. Tests are a technological device that, combined with an effective policy and public-health bureaucracy for its distribution, allows us to stop the spread of a virus.[5]

At a broad level, tests have value because they can lead to better decisions to reduce the spread of the virus. Without tests, individuals, households, and businesses must incur the costs associated with treating every individual as someone equally likely to be infected and contagious.

A couple of months back, Ajay Agrawal, Avi Goldfarb, and Mara Lederman, and I explained that when everyone is equally risky to others, location managers have to invest in "always on" solutions. Here was our description:

> All sorts of decisions that previously would have been made on the basis of productivity and efficiency now need to also consider the possibility of infection. In the restaurant industry, the flow of people in and out of the kitchen is now an infection-risk management problem. In the retail fashion industry, decisions about whether to open changing rooms or allow

---

[5]   John Cochrane, "Tests," (The Grumpy Economist, August 20, 2020), https://johnhcochrane.blogspot.com/2020/08/tests.html.

customers to try items on are now infection-risk management problems. Moving from physical to digital documents now reduces infection risk as well increasing efficiency and wasting less paper. The risk of transferring the virus by exchanging cash increases the relative benefits of digital payment systems.

To date, we have seen two broad types of always-on solutions. The first kind do not change the number or nature of interactions but aim to make those interactions less risky. Things like masks, hand sanitizer stations, and plexiglass screens at reception desks and store checkouts all fall into this category.

The second kind are solutions that aim to make people interact less. These include redesigned physical spaces (to minimize interactions or high-touch surfaces), redesigned workflows (to enable work to be done in parallel or sequence rather than jointly), and redesigned people-management processes (to minimize interactions across groups or teams). Reductions in capacity—whether of employees (through layoffs and furloughs) or customers (through limits on occupancy)—fall into this category as well.

Always-on solutions impose additional costs on business. There are direct costs for things like protective equipment and more frequent cleaning. If the always-on solution involves reduced capacity, profits will fall. Finally, reengineered spaces, workflows, and processes may lead to lower productivity, greater inefficiency, or unhappier workers. Of course, certain changes could increase productivity. Some businesses, especially those in congested cities like New York, report that work from home has made them more productive, mainly because it eliminates long commutes.

Different types of businesses lend themselves differently to always-on solutions. It's easier to maintain social distancing in garden centers than in hair salons. Some businesses are choosing not to open even if they are allowed to. Many restaurants have elected to keep their dine-in services closed because with social distancing, they can't allow in enough customers at a time to offset the costs of cleaners and wait staff.[6]

Depending on the business, the costs of having an always-on solution can be different. When costs are high, there is greater value to finding a way to identify people who are more likely to be infected and then use that information to protect others rather than treating everyone as equally dangerous. Schools are places where these costs have become significant. Even with stringent health measures, the educational experience has significantly declined. The negative impact on education reminds us that the cost of always-on solutions is not just about dollar expenditures, but also about social and generational costs. As the pandemic hangs over our heads, we need to consider better solutions.

If we focus only on the economic impact of the pandemic, an economy-wide picture reveals a stark perspective. Estimates of Covid-19's cost to the global economy vary, but it could be many hundreds of billions of dollars *per week*. The economic damage could be significantly reduced with the right solutions. One study showed that by using a comprehensive screening system in the US, on the order of 630,000 screens per day among a random sample of the population, the savings to the monthly GDP would be more than half a trillion dollars (while preventing more than 150,000 deaths).[7] That return on investment is ten times greater than the expected cost of the screens. Even if we ignore the economy-wide benefit, this is a project with a 300 percent rate of return for the government alone. In other words, it is deficit reducing. It is difficult to imagine a more worthwhile strategy.

---

[6]   Ajay Agrawal, Joshua Gans, Avi Goldfarb, and Mara Lederman, "The CEO's Guide to Safely Reopening the Workplace," *MIT Technology Review*, May 28, 2020, https://www.technologyreview.com/2020/05/28/1002326/business-workplace-reopening-safely-testing-covid-19.

[7]   Andrew Atkeson, Michael Droste, Michael Mina, and James H. Stock, "Economic Benefits of Covid-19 Screening Tests," (medRxiv, 2020). See also R. Cherif and F. Hasanov, "A TIP Against the COVID-19 Pandemic," (IMF Working Paper 20/114).

Matching Information to Purpose

A test is a means of gathering information needed to make better decisions. Thus, we must clearly articulate the nature of the decisions we need to make before we advocate for or develop a test. Indeed, a theme that runs throughout this book is that information must be matched to its purpose.

With regard to testing for the presence of a coronavirus like Covid-19, four broad decisions could improve testing outcomes.[8]

- Diagnosis: whether to treat or monitor a particular patient for coronavirus complications
- Clearance: whether to allow someone to interact with others in a close physical setting, such as when a patient is being treated by a health professional, or during travel
- Mitigation: whether to isolate someone from other people
- Surveillance: whether to engage in non-health interventions to prevent the spread of disease

For each of these decisions, knowing if someone is infected is valuable information that can prompt actions that can lead to varied consequences. Each of the options listed above also depends on whether tests are cheap and widely available, whether the tests provide accurate results, and whether test results can be received quickly.

The focus in this book is on the *non-diagnostic* reasons for testing and screening. For example, the *clearance* approach was adopted early as a screening system, especially by professional sports leagues. The NBA set up a bubble at Walt Disney World in Orlando, Florida, in July 2020. All players, coaches, and staff members were required to live in the bubble. This involved a quarantine and other strict protocols, but the virus was kept out. To

---

[8]   These are based on categories identified by Carl Bergstrom. Source: https://www.slideshare.net/Carl_Bergstrom/proactive-covid19-testing-to-mitigate-spread.

avoid those costs, Major League Baseball chose to test players and staff every other day. That allowed the season to continue, complete with travel.[9] To be sure, the MLB's favorable outcome was aided by the fact that baseball is an outdoor sport. That said, the National Hockey League also had similar positive outcomes. Both cases demonstrate that testing can substitute for more drastic and costly protection measures. As we will see, similar clearance approaches to testing have assisted in reopening college campuses without serious outbreaks.

The real benefit, however, occurs with *mitigation*, which addresses the core of the pandemic information gap. By identifying and isolating infectious people, the transmission chains of Covid-19 can be broken. By keeping the number of cases to a minimum, there is a reduced need for the harsher measures (e.g., lockdowns) designed to prevent hospitals from reaching capacity (flattening the curve). In fact, when the prevalence of disease becomes low enough, the mitigation testing strategy can eventually eradicate the virus from a population. Some countries, such as South Korea, successfully achieved this outcome, but because the virus is still circulating in other countries, full eradication and post-pandemic normality has not been possible.

Even apart from choices to use the clearance and mitigation options, gathering information is a critical aspect of surveillance. Countries often have to impose lockdowns in a wide area because they cannot locate where outbreaks are occurring in the mass of aggregate case numbers. Constant monitoring, which is possible through various means, can provide that information to governments. Proper surveillance can enable governments to deploy targeted rather than widespread interventions.

---

[9]   Will Leitch, "The Pandemic Lessons from MLB's Surprisingly Successful Season," *New York Magazine*, October 20, 2020, https://nymag.com/intelligencer/2020/10/pandemic-lessons-from-mlbs-surprisingly-successful-season.html.

The Plan for This Book

This book will provide an in-depth discussion of the main issues and trade-offs associated with various methods by which information can be gathered to help plug pandemic information gaps. In chapter 2, we look more closely at tests and, in particular, at the information they can reveal to inform decision-making. We want high quality Covid-19 tests that, as a matter of standard, give us information in a way that is similar to the information we get from the visible symptoms of different viral infections, such as SARS. As an illustration in *The Pandemic Information Gap*, I imagined a virus that caused the noses of people who contracted it to light up, bright red, like Rudolph the Red-Nosed Reindeer. In that scenario, it would be easy to clear locations and mitigate the spread of the virus by isolating people with red noses until their noses returned to normal. Unfortunately, in the real world, we must rely on trade-offs because we do not have perfect ability to see infected people. We have tests that are quite accurate, but not perfect. That fact matters for how decisions are made.

To better understand Covid-19 tests, I introduce the concepts of sensitivity and specificity. The tests that have been predominantly used to detect Covid-19 are called PCR tests. They are classified as high-sensitivity tests because they will accurately signal a positive detection of the virus when the virus is present, and they will fail to detect the presence of the virus when the virus is not there.

However, the problem with these tests is that they were designed and approved for diagnostic testing; that is, to inform the decision of whether to treat someone for Covid-19. To solve the pandemic information problem, we need a test that will tell us whether someone is *infectious* and not simply infected with the coronavirus. PCR tests can provide information about infectiousness, but typically they are not used for that purpose. As it turns out, a different sort of test—an antigen test—can provide a more accurate signal of whether someone is infectious. In contrast to PCR tests, which can detect the virus even if it is already dead, antigen tests work best when an individual has a high viral load and is likely to be infectious. Thus, an antigen test provides higher specificity for infectiousness than a PCR test. From the perspective of actual infectiousness, a PCR test generates many false positives and, due to its high sensitivity, many false negatives. The result is, therefore, a reduced ability to isolate infectious people.

Antigen tests have two other significant advantages over PCR tests. First, they are much cheaper, costing about $5 as opposed to $100 per test. Second, they produce results much faster—in five to fifteen minutes as opposed to eight hours, a day, or longer due to the lab processing required for PCR tests. Thus, as is shown in chapter 3, antigen tests can be deployed more widely to test asymptomatic people. They provide information that better enables us to find those with or without "red-nose" symptoms and, therefore, more frequently ensure that the chains of transmission are broken. Antigen tests can serve as *screens* that allow us to systematically sort infectious and non-infectious people. They are a much, much better temperature check.

To really deal with Covid-19, however, we need to do more than administer screens. We also need a sustainable screening system. Once-off interventions can find infectious people and isolate them. But the potential reductions in the prevalence of Covid-19 would be short-lived. To obtain true economic benefits from screens, we need a system that works in an ongoing manner. Chapter 4 describes the challenges that such a system would need to overcome in order to function at scale. These challenges would include: *reducing the costs* of delivering and implementing screens; *improving convenience* to ensure that people can be screened with minimal sacrifice; and *behavioral interventions* to ensure that people comply with recommendations and do not end up creating more viral spread.

Chapter 5 focuses on data requirements for surveillance. In particular, it is shown that population-level data can be collected from wastewater and that by using artificial intelligence, it is possible to get early warning of outbreaks even at a block-by-block level. By having more information about the networks of interactions among people, some of which could be collected at non-pandemic times, it would be possible to have more targeted and less widespread interventions (e.g., lockdowns) and other interventions to deal with outbreaks. All of this would reduce the economic costs of pandemic management.

Pandemic management also depends on how individuals manage their own risk. Chapter 6 explores this aspect of the pandemic information solution. It involves providing people with more information about disease prevalence, especially within their own networks. That knowledge can allow people to adjust their behavior so as to mitigate risks. There is evidence that personal risk management has, in many ways, had a strong impact on reducing the extent of Covid-19 outbreaks.

Chapter 7 addresses the other information tool at the disposal of public health authorities: contact tracing. Tracing contacts is a means of getting ahead of the virus by identifying who might have been exposed to an infectious person. But contact tracing can also be effectively used to find out who gave the virus to an infected person. Tracing efforts have been shown to have large impacts on infection rates even when disease prevalence is relatively high. Tracing strategies have proved essential in countries where Covid-19 prevalence has been held virtually at zero.

Finally, chapter 8 offers some thoughts about the institutions that might be needed in the future to ensure we can manage the pandemic information problem during future pandemics.

What about Vaccines?

In November 2020, the first studies showing the efficacy of Covid-19 vaccines appeared, giving us some rare positive news and representing an unprecedented speed of vaccine development. By the end of the year, three vaccine candidates had been approved in the United Kingdom and elsewhere. By January 2020, Israel had inoculated over a quarter of its population and was on track to vaccinate the entire population in March. Given all of this, it is natural to ask whether solutions to the pandemic information problem are still relevant?

I wish we were done, or soon to be done, with Covid-19. However, the vaccination solution still has some major challenges. First, it will likely take several years to manufacture and distribute Covid-19 vaccines globally, at least to a degree that provides herd immunity (the threshold level of immunity in a population that naturally prevents viral outbreaks). Even more time will likely be needed to eliminate the pandemic. From that perspective, at the beginning of 2021, we are not even halfway through this crisis.

Second, there is a lot we do not know about the vaccines. Vaccine immunity may not be long-lasting, which means the virus might reemerge. Also, although the vaccines provide effective immunity (protecting individuals from the harmful effects of the coronavirus), we do not know if they provide sterilizing immunity, which is the ability to stop vaccinated people from spreading the virus. Some vaccines—such as for HPV and the measles—do this, but others do not. There is reason for optimism on this front, but to work out these questions will require continued testing and vigilance. Again, these troublesome realities will extend the economic and social consequences of Covid-19.

Finally, and more worrying, is the future. Viruses mutate. Mutations could dodge the vaccines. This is why influenza remains a problem and why the remnants of the 1918 pandemic are still with us in our bouts with the annual seasonal flu.

> Importantly, it is possible that this virus could mutate at any moment. And it could mutate around the vaccine derived immunity. All of the leading vaccines are narrow scope single protein vaccines. Unfortunately, all four of the leading vaccines

for use in the US are essentially identical—so not only are the vaccines themselves narrow in scope, but the entire vaccine program, the whole basket of vaccines is narrow in scope. That means we need just a single virus particle, somewhere out there in the world to learn how to evade the narrow single protein derived immunity of the vaccine to render the vaccines potentially useless or at least much less powerful. This should have been a major consideration long ago, but it wasn't and still is barely a talking point. No one wants to talk about this real risk.[10]

For these reasons, we need tests and information solutions.

These tests will be "immune" to such changes in the virus and can induce herd effects through empowering people to know their status and thus help people to not transmit the virus to their loved ones.[11]

Vaccines help by giving us reasons for optimism. But it takes time and there are risks. To mitigate those risks and to shorten the economic and social consequences of Covid-19, we must continue to work toward finding pandemic information solutions. The returns of that work will be high.

---

[10] Michael Mina as quoted by Emily Oster, "Antigen Testing," (Parent Data, January 7, 2021), https://emilyoster.substack.com/p/antigen-testing-guest-post-with-michael.

[11] Ibid.

2
Information from Tests

Sometimes a virus exposes the solution. With the SARS coronavirus, which had a major outbreak in 2003, patients developed symptoms a day or so before they were infectious. This meant that anyone with symptoms could be quickly isolated. As a result, the pandemic was over in six months or so. MERS, in 2015, exhibited a similar pattern. That potential pandemic ended in just two months. Symptoms are the "tell" of a virus. When they are associated with infectiousness, we can then act.

SARS-CoV-2, the novel coronavirus that appeared in 2019, can spread asymptomatically. People who develop symptoms can be infectious and spread the virus a day or so before those symptoms appear. It is also possible that infected people can have mild or no symptoms at all. In other words, this virus has a limited "tell." Importantly, that means that it does not carry its own solution to the information problem. Like HIV, it can spread silently.

For a virus looking to spread within human society, silent spreading is an evolutionary pinnacle. What that means is that we must actively solve the information problem. Fortunately, science has presented us with the means to do that: test populations widely at the outset.

That testing can be used as a critical tool to fight pandemics is well recognized. In the case of Covid-19, some countries went to great lengths to ensure that a testing infrastructure was in place. Even as early as March 2020, some people were calling for widespread testing to identify asymptomatic carriers and then isolate them quickly. Among those was Paul Romer, a Nobel laureate in economics and someone prone to think big when it is required.[12] He wasn't alone. Romer was joined by other economists[13] and Harvard infectious disease professor Michael Mina. Indeed, in my previous book, I imagined a "testing economy" whereby cheap tests could be applied as a way of life throughout the pandemic. This vision was not taken up by the US even though funding was allocated by Congress to ramp up testing. The US response was not unique. No country where the pandemic raged out of control opted to implement widespread testing. This suggests a deeper resistance.

It is not my task here to explore that resistance. At the time of this writing, I see that resistance waning, but I have no strong insight into it. I will offer some hints in what follows, but my goal in this chapter and the next is to lay out a comprehensive case for widespread testing as a way of managing pandemics and their economic consequences. In this chapter, I will focus on testing that is used primarily for diagnostic purposes. In the next, I will focus on screening systems that use different testing instruments to enable a fully operational testing economy.

The Gold Standard for Testing

When radar was invented during World War II, there was an

---

[12] Paul Romer and Alan M. Garber, "Will Our Economy Die from Coronavirus," *The New York Times*, March 23, 2020, https://www.nytimes.com/2020/03/23/opinion/coronavirus-depression.html; Isaac Chotiner, "Paul Romer's Case for Nationwide Coronavirus Testing," *The New Yorker*, May 3, 2020, https://www.newyorker.com/news/q-and-a/paul-romer-on-how-to-survive-the-chaos-of-the-coronavirus.

[13] For example, Alex Tabarrok, "Mass Testing to Fix the Labor Market," (Marginal Revolution, March 20, 2020), https://marginalrevolution.com/marginalrevolution/2020/03/when-and-how-we-can-go-back-to-work.html.

immediate problem. If operators saw an object on a radar screen, how could they know if it represented an enemy plane or a flock of birds (noise)? When targets were farther away from the radar, more noise could potentially appear on the screen. Operators had to decide whether to sound an alarm. Two errors were possible: sound an alarm when there was no real target (false alarm) or not sound an alarm when there was a real danger (missed target). It is no surprise that, in a military situation, the costs of a miss were greater than the costs of a false alarm, and so radar operators were told to err on the side of caution.

It would be a great world if we had perfect tests for the presence of the coronavirus. Then we would know who is infected or not, and we would be able to act accordingly. But testing errors cause us to worry about how often those errors arise and also about the relative costs of different errors. These concerns are made all the more important because, in the design of any test, we make choices regarding the mix of errors that might arise. We presume that actions resulting from a test will be straightforward; that is, if someone is positive, then we isolate and treat them, and if he or she is negative, then we relax. In other words, we ask of our tests for a straight up-or-down result when, in fact, we end up throwing away important information discovered by the tests.

The gold standard for testing is the PCR test, or "reverse-transcription polymerase chain reaction" test. It is quite amazing. Invented in 1983, it made the Human Genome Project possible and netted biochemist Kary Mullis a Nobel Prize a decade later. Here is how it works.

> It works, in essence, like a zoom-and-enhance feature on a computer: Using a specific mix of chemicals, called "reagents," and a special machine, called a "thermal cycler," the PCR process duplicates a certain strand of genetic material hundreds of millions of times.

> When used to test for Covid-19, the PCR technique looks

for a specific sequence of nucleotides that is unique to the coronavirus, a snippet of RNA that exists nowhere else. Whenever the PCR machine—as designed and sold, for instance, by the multinational firm Roche—encounters that strand, it makes a copy of both that sequence and a fluorescent dye. If, after multiplying both the strand and the dye hundreds of millions of times, the Roche machine detects a certain amount of the dye, its software interprets the specimen as a positive. To have a 'confirmed case of Covid-19' is to have a PCR machine detect the dye in a sample and report it to a technician. Tested time and time again, the PCR technique performs stunningly well: The best-in-class PCR tests can reliably detect, in just a few hours, as few as one hundred copies of viral RNA in a milliliter of spit or snot.[14]

This process is important because it provides a measure of the *viral load* of the coronavirus. To find the needle in the haystack that is SARS-CoV-2 RNA, the process takes a strand and replicates it in a cycle. After each cycle, the machine looks for the required amount of dye that would indicate the presence of some of the RNA. If a sample has a high viral load, then that point might be reached in five cycles. If it has a low viral load, it might take more than thirty-five cycles. As a cycle is part of exponential growth, a Ct (or cycle count) score of five is many orders of magnitude lower than a Ct of thirty-five. The number of cycles taken is, therefore, a measure of the amount of virus present in the sample.

Interestingly, this means that a negative test, that is when the "presence of SARS-CoV-2 is not confirmed," it means that a given number cycles occurred without triggering enough RNA to be detected. How many cycles? Forty is the usual threshold. Why is that the threshold? Because this process is essentially an optimal stopping rule issue; in other words, the more you look, the longer

---

the process takes. Even with more cycles, we can never be 100 percent sure the virus is not present in small amounts. In other words, this, like many other tests, is a statistical process.

Given this rap, it is not surprising that most government health authorities use this measure as the testing standard, and it is why the majority of Covid-19 tests used thus far have been PCR tests. But nothing good comes for free. These tests are expensive—between $50 and $150 a person—and they rely on machines and reagents that have also run into supply chain limitations during the pandemic.

Even with all of that accuracy, the test process is not perfect. First of all, a person can be infected with coronavirus and not have a positive test result. This is especially the case in the first couple of days after the virus enters the body. As it replicates throughout the body, it doesn't immediately show up in the nasal passages. By day three, however, the PCR test can pick up the genetic remnants of the virus in nasal passages or saliva. But, assuming a person develops symptoms at all, these genetic remnants won't show up for a couple of days. So, between days three and five, a person can be infectious or contagious without knowing it—unless he or she happens to have a test during that time. And another thing—which we will address more in chapter 3—is that even if a person has a test on day three, it might take a day or two to get the results. So, there is almost no hope of using a PCR test to catch people early and isolate them.

That said, in the case of asymptomatic individuals, there could still be more time to pick someone out and do some good—if we encouraged asymptomatic people to be tested. Unfortunately, given the cost of the tests, asymptomatic people are not encouraged to get tests, and they are not given priority for speedy results. Therein lies the problem with a gold standard test. It offers high quality, but it also imposes high expenditures that lead everyone involved to seek more economical approaches.

The problems don't stop after the first week of contracting the virus. We are learning that after about fourteen days, the coronavirus has finished its damage in causing Covid-19.[15] This is actually great news because the virus in the body is inactive and can no longer do damage to others. However, the PCR test is designed to detect the virus, whether dead or alive. In other words, a person can still test positive—because he or she is still infected with inactive virus—but without being infectious or contagious. Thus, it would be wrong at best and misleading at worst to use PCR tests to inform decisions about isolation and contact tracing.

South Korea

Having been scared and scarred by MERS in 2015, suffering thirty-eight deaths, South Korea was extremely prepared for a potential pandemic. My focus here is on what they prioritized during that preparation.

It started on January 20, 2020. That was the day South Korea identified its first case of Covid-19. (The US also identified its first case on that day). The outbreak quickly spread, with over three thousand confirmed cases by the end of February. This was a pattern similar to other countries. But at this point, South Korea's path diverged from other nations. Case numbers started to fall dramatically (see figure 2.1) because South Korea was prepared.

When the novel coronavirus was first identified on December 31, 2019, several things swung into action. Top of the list was the development of a diagnostic test. This was done by identifying the RNA candidates and then building a PCR kit for that purpose. South Korea did not wait for the test's efficacy to be verified before

---

[15] Seungjae Lee, Tark Kim, Eunjung Lee, et al., "Clinical Course and Molecular Viral Shedding Among Asymptomatic and Symptomatic Patients With SARS-CoV-2 Infection in a Community Treatment Center in the Republic of Korea," *JAMA Internal Medicine* 180, no. 11, (2020):1447–1452, doi:10.1001/jamainternmed.2020.3862, https://jamanetwork.com/journals/jamainternalmedicine/fullarticle/2769235.

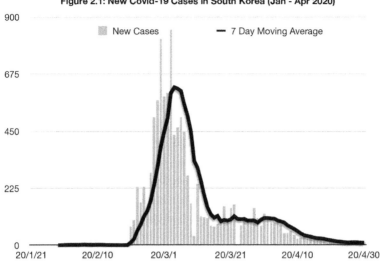

Figure 2.1: New Covid-19 Cases in South Korea (Jan - Apr 2020)

Source: ourworldindata.org (https://github.com/owid/covid-19-data/tree/master/public/data), accessed December 28, 2020.

starting to manufacture thousands of test kits and then distributing them to hospitals. On day one after the test's efficacy was established, they were able to begin widespread testing.

The effects were immediate. One woman, who became known as Patient 31, was quickly diagnosed. Critically, her movements were also documented (more on this aspect of information in chapter 4). It turned out that she had attended a megachurch in the city of Daegu in mid-February. South Korea was in a position to find and test all congregants. They were tested regardless of whether they had symptoms. The testing effort discovered 5,080 cases connected to that one event.[16] Across the country, in March, South Korea tested twelve thousand people a day on average (twenty thousand on peak days). In total (let alone per capita) they did more testing than any other country (see figure 2.2).

---

[16] Youjin Shin, Bonnie Berkowitz, and Min Joo Kim, "How a South Korean Church Helped Fuel the Spread of the Coronavirus," *The Washington Post*, March 25, 2020, https://www.washingtonpost.com/graphics/2020/world/coronavirus-south-korea-church/.

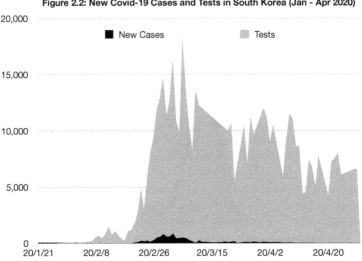

Figure 2.2: New Covid-19 Cases and Tests in South Korea (Jan - Apr 2020)

We should note several important things about the South Korean response. First, testing rates were high but testing was not widespread. Indeed, South Korea aggressively pursued testing in regions where there were outbreaks. This helped them stop those outbreaks from spreading to other regions and kept numbers low everywhere. Second, South Korea's authorities knew that Covid-19 had highly variable transmission and that many outbreaks were the result of super-spreading events, such as the church gathering in Daegu.[17] Being able to test and trace allowed South Korean authorities to identify those events, which made locating infected people easier. Finally, throughout this period, South Korea was able to avoid aggressive lockdowns. It's true that the population reduced its social interactions and activities, as measured by mobility data (on the order of 10 to 20 percent for certain activities). It's also true that the population was agreeable to wearing masks. But the economic hardships in South Korea were less severe compared to

---

[17] For instance, this pattern appears in many countries. A. Hasan, H. Susanto, M.F. Kasim et al., "Superspreading in Early Transmissions of Covid-19 in Indonesia, *Scientific Reports* 10, 22386, (December 28, 2020), https://doi.org/10.1038/s41598-020-79352-5.

other places (e.g., Italy and Spain) where aggressive lockdowns curtailed economic activity by 80 to 90 percent.

In other words, having a testing infrastructure in place to be deployed at the beginning of a potential pandemic shielded South Korea from the worst health and economic effects of the pandemic.

That said, South Korea did face problems during the crisis, which required innovation. In the early months, the demand for tests could often outstrip supply. But the development, for instance, of testing booths made it possible to increase by ninefold the throughput of testing centers.[18] The booths made it possible to protect health care professionals who administered the test without the need for changes in protective clothing between test subjects.

Sensitivity Versus Specificity

The South Korean example shows how PCR testing could play a critical role in containing a viral outbreak at an early stage. But, as already noted, PCR testing is expensive, it requires trained health personnel to collect the samples, and it requires labs to process the results. For economists, the question is whether those costs are worth it. The standard answer is that PCR tests offer high quality. But there are always trade-offs. Thus, we need to understand what that high quality is buying us in terms of outcomes.

For a medical diagnosis, the efficacy of tests is characterized by the concepts of sensitivity and specificity. The *sensitivity* of a test is the probability that someone who has Covid-19 tests positive for Covid-19. You would like that probability to be close to 100 percent. The *specificity* of a test is the probability that someone who does not have Covid-19 tests negative for Covid-19. You would like

---

[18] Sang Il Kim and Ji Yong Lee, "Walk-Through Screening Center for Covid-19: An Accessible and Efficient Screening System in a Pandemic Situation," *Journal of Korean Medical Science* 35, no. 15, (April 14, 2020), https://doi.org/10.3346/jkms.2020.35.e154.

this probability to be close to 1. The issue is that there is another choice variable inherent in a test with two outcomes (i.e., positive or negative): What is the threshold by which the outcome of a test is defined as positive if that threshold is exceeded and negative if it is not? Change the threshold and you potentially alter the sensitivity and specificity of a test—in opposite directions.

Before going into this, it might be useful to calibrate the terminology here. Recall that statistical inference of testing came out of signal detection theory for radars. In that case, radar operators were worried about false alarms (thinking there was a hostile plane when there was not) and misses (failing to detect a hostile plane). In 1947, Jacob Yerushalmy realized that this same dilemma arose in medical diagnosis that relied on X-rays. He wrote:

> The object of the analysis is to obtain measures for the relative efficiency of the different X-ray techniques in selecting the individuals in the study group who have X-ray evidence suggestive of tuberculosis. The usual procedure is to determine for each of the four techniques two measures:
>
> 1. A measure of sensitivity or the probability of correct diagnosis of "positive" cases, and
>
> 2. A measure of specificity or the probability of correct diagnosis of "negative" cases.[19]

Yerushalmy did not explain why he chose those words, but they stuck for medicine. In other situations, when evaluating tests or predictions, people tend to focus on errors. So, whereas sensitivity is the number of true positives divided by the number of positives (or the number of true positives plus the number of false negatives), others measure the number of false negatives as something that everyone wishes was lower. Similarly, whereas specificity is the

---

[19] Jacob Yerushalmy, "Statistical Problems in Assessing Methods of Medical Diagnosis, with Special Reference to X-Ray Techniques," *Public Health Reports* 62, no. 40, (Oct. 3, 1947): 1432-1449, https://www.jstor.org/stable/4586294.

number of true negatives divided by the number of negatives, others measure the number of false positives as something to be minimized. They are the same concepts, but they are placed in a (ahem) positive or negative light.

Here is my conjecture for where the term *sensitivity* originates. In the context of medical diagnosis, the meaning of sensitivity is akin to image resolution. How clear is an X-ray image? How easy is it to find an RNA remnant in a sample? If a highly sensitive test can detect small amounts of something, it has a higher resolution. In other words, a highly sensitive instrument can trigger a positive test result even when the thing is hardly there. In the case of *specificity,* a negative result is recorded only after someone searches extensively for the thing and eventually gives up; that is, after attempting to leave no stone unturned. There is a belief that for both sensitivity and specificity, more effort can improve outcomes. But due to limits on effort and time, there must be a trade-off.

PCR tests are favored because they have sensitivity and specificity that both lie above certain thresholds. In particular, the sensitivity of PCR tests has been measured at 71 to 98 percent (akin to false-negative rates of 2 to 29 percent). If some of those numbers seem high, it is because PCR tests involve two steps, and the second step involves a machine to find the RNA in the sample. During the first step, a health worker inserts a swab far into the nose to hunt for evidence of the virus. Not surprisingly, there might be variation in how well that hunt goes, but done well, the sensitivity can be quite high.

In the case of specificity, a commonly used number for PCR tests is 95 percent; in other words, there are few false positives. Some have argued that the specificity is more like 99.5 percent.[20] Regardless, if a PCR test comes back negative—at least insofar

---

[20] John Otter, "Testing Patients and Staff Without Symptoms for SARS-CoV-2: Beware False-Positives (and Negatives)," (Reflections on Infection Protection and Control, May 21, 2020), https://reflectionsipc.com/2020/05/21/screening-patients-and-staff-without-symptoms-for-sars-cov-2-beware-false-positives-and-negatives.

as RNA remnants are concerned—then the result is conclusively negative.

However, as I mentioned earlier, PCR tests find RNA remnants—inactive or active. And, over the course of even symptomatic infections, the time a virus is dead can outstrip the time it is alive.

This is very important because the PCR test is used as a benchmark (or gold standard) by which all other tests are assessed. In other words, when researchers examine the efficacy of some other test for Covid-19, they examine the outcomes in relation to the PCR test. If the non-PCR test *disagrees* with the PCR test, the non-PCR test will be seen as having inferior sensitivity and specificity. Even if the PCR test is wrong and the other test is right, the other test would be scored with lower marks! Suffice it to say, this is quite the game. To me, it seems like those Jim Crow era voting eligibility tests that required people to guess the number of jellybeans in a jar. The correct response is: By what standard?

It actually gets worse. You may wonder, by what standard did the evaluators of these tests calculate the sensitivity and specificity of PCR tests? The answer is, by conducting other PCR tests! This is a problematic form of circular reasoning.

We can see that PCR tests are considered to have high specificity (low false positives) and less high sensitivity (more false negatives). From a diagnostic perspective, this might make some sense. No one wants to use up a hospital bed or treat someone who does not have Covid-19 but instead has the flu. These scenarios can "do harm" and doctors have a motto against that.

Perfect Is the Enemy of the Good

High sensitivity and specificity are the reasons why PCR tests are favored by medical professionals and public health regulators.

However, adhering to high quality can involve critical trade-offs. One example of how this played out was with respect to the US roll-out of testing kits in February 2020. As this example shows, the perfect can become the enemy of the good.

Like South Korea's, the US playbook involved quickly rolling out testing as part of the strategy to contain outbreaks and minimize spread. Within three days of the first confirmed US case, the Centers for Disease Control and Prevention (CDC) shared details of a test it had designed. The CDC's intention was to manufacture and distribute its own testing kits. But faced with capacity issues, it restricted those who could be tested to those who had recently travelled to Wuhan or had been in direct contact with an infected person. At the time, there were only small numbers of either. Nonetheless, many labs could apply to conduct the relevant PCR tests.[21] The restrictions on testing were really only lifted in March.

This, however, was far from the only constraint. A problem quickly emerged. The initial test kits manufactured and distributed by the CDC were "flawed" and did not work as intended. The reagents for one part of the tests had issues, making them unreliable. A CDC spokesperson in late February articulated their policy: "We obviously would not want to use anything but the most perfect possible kits, since we're making determinations about whether people have Covid-19 or not."[22]

It is interesting to look at the part that failed. There were three genetic sequences in the PCR tests. The first two were for genetic markers of the novel coronavirus. The final one was used to rule out other known coronaviruses. That was the part that failed. But, as a result, no testing could be conducted for a month. In retrospect,

---

[21] Meg Kelly, Sarah Cahlan, and Elyse Samuels, "What Went Wrong with Coronavirus Testing in the US," *The Washington Post*, March 30, 2020, https://www.washingtonpost.com/politics/2020/03/30/11-100000-what-went-wrong-with-coronavirus-testing-us.

[22] Robert P. Baird, "What Went Wrong with Coronavirus Testing in the U.S.," *The New Yorker,* March 26, 2020, https://www.newyorker.com/news/news-desk/what-went-wrong-with-coronavirus-testing-in-the-us.

this seems extraordinary. After all, the tests could detect whether the novel coronavirus was present. The third part was simply a confirmation for other coronaviruses.

Eventually, the CDC relented.

> In a maddening update on February 26, the CDC informed public labs that they could go ahead and run their original test kits—and simply disregard the problematic third prong. The original diagnostic tests, in other words, had been reliable all along. Frieden, the former CDC director, remains incredulous at how this unfolded: 'It took them three weeks to say, "Just don't use the third component!"'[23]

The CDC had designed a test and had hoped it would be perfect and clear. When one of the nonessential components didn't work, they could have adjusted instructions for how to read the test, but instead the CDC placed a hold on all testing. A desire for the perfect was the enemy of the good.

Mistakes will be made in a crisis. There will be manufacturing challenges and a need to adjust course. But decision-makers must be willing to adjust. For whatever reason, that did not occur at the CDC during February 2020. As I will argue in what follows, this same reluctance to move from what was purported to be "best practice" also hampered many countries' pandemic responses throughout 2020.

Pooled Testing

Supply constraints plagued many countries as they rolled out PCR testing. It was often easy to collect samples from people (subject to having the right nasal swabs on hand), but there were

---

[23] Tim Dickinson, "The Four Men Responsible for America's Covid-19 Test Disaster," *Rolling Stone*, May 10, 2020, https://www.rollingstone.com/politics/politics-features/covid-19-test-trump-admin-failed-disaster-995930/.

limits to how many samples could be processed by labs and, at times, limits on the reagents used to process those tests. These supply constraints had two big effects. First, they caused governments to restrict testing to symptomatic patients or those who had direct exposures to an infected person. In other words, there was little capacity to test for asymptomatic transmission and to get ahead of the pandemic information gap. Second, supply constraints caused a slowdown in the system. Rather than taking less than a day to generate results after people were swabbed, it often took many days or a week for those results to come through. As will be discussed in the next chapter, those delays meant that the tests were virtually useless for pandemic control. As Bill Gates later remarked: "The majority of all US tests are completely garbage, wasted."[24]

To speed things up, countries could rely more on an old idea from the HIV era: pooled (or group) testing. For example, a testing lab could divide the samples taken from one hundred people into four groups of twenty-five. The samples of each group would be pooled together and then tested collectively (four tests). If one collective sample showed the presence of Covid-19, the twenty-five people in that group would be tested individually (twenty-five more tests). Overall, in this scenario, only twenty-nine tests would be needed rather than one hundred tests. Given that only 1 or 2 percent of people tested are infected, this approach would save considerable time and resources.[25] Of course, if prevalence is higher, then the value of pooled testing is reduced.

It could actually be even better than that. Mathematicians have shown how to test pools of samples to identify infected people without any individual testing. Instead of running one test on a pool

[24] Steve Levy, "Bill Gates on Covid: Most US Tests Are 'Completely Garbage,'" *Wired*, August 8, 2020, https://www.wired.com/story/bill-gates-on-covid-most-us-tests-are-completely-garbage/.

[25] Christopher D Pilcher, Daniel Westreich, Michael G Hudgens, "Group Testing for Severe Acute Respiratory Syndrome–Coronavirus 2 to Enable Rapid Scale-Up of Testing and Real-Time Surveillance of Incidence," *The Journal of Infectious Diseases* 222, no. 6, (September 15, 2020): 903–909, https://doi.org/10.1093/infdis/jiaa378.

of twenty-five samples, ten tests would be conducted on overlapping groups.[26] These methods, however, would likely require additional automation to implement properly.

Nonetheless, such a process is invaluable if you want to test large numbers of people quickly. In May 2020, Wuhan, China, which was the first place in the world to suffer from a significant Covid-19 outbreak, was nearing the end of a very harsh lockdown. Cases were low, but to reopen the city, health officials wanted to be sure that cases were not lurking and still circulating. They embarked on an ambitious plan to test the entire city's population of ten million people in just two weeks.

They found three hundred positive cases, all asymptomatic. What's more, they found no infections among 1,174 close contacts of the infected.[27] By using pooled testing, health workers increased the number of tests from forty-seven thousand per day to over a million. Wuhan reopened and by summer was operating with few restrictions.

Driving Costs Lower

There are other ways to reduce the costs associated with PCR testing. A major cost in both dollars and time is having to use a lab to process test results. This has given rise to various point-of-care options, which also have the advantage of generating faster results. One example is Abbott's ID Now solution,[28] which uses an on-location machine. (It was used by the White House). There are also other solutions, such as the Detect test by Homodeus and the

---

[26] Smriti Mallapaty, "The Mathematical Strategy That Could Transform Coronavirus Testing," *Nature* 583, (July 10, 2020): 504-505, https://doi.org/10.1038/d41586-020-02053-6.

[27] Shiyi Cao, Yong Gan, Chao Wang, et al., "Post-Lockdown SARS-CoV-2 Nucleic Acid Screening in Nearly Ten Million Residents of Wuhan, China," *Nature Communications* 11, 5917 (2020), https://doi.org/10.1038/s41467-020-19802-w.

[28] Abbott, https://www.abbott.com/IDNOW/IDNOW-COVID-19-FAQ.html.

Personal PCR test by Visby Medical. These single-use methods aim to offer PCR tests without a dedicated machine.

The goal of these initiatives is to develop tests that allow us to have our cake and eat it too. This is what Jonathan Rothberg, who is behind Homodeus, argues.

> Rothberg, who is sensitive to the criticism that his own innovations are merely low-rent versions of better technologies, was determined in this case to make no compromises. His product would not only do away with the machines required by his competitors' antigen tests, it would approximate the diagnostic rigor of the PCR standard. The FDA's willingness to relax its benchmark for rapid tests was, he felt, irrelevant; he liked to quote the old Hebrew National slogan, 'We answer to a higher authority.'[29]

So Rothberg's approach is to match the PCR test by going for a no-compromise solution. Meanwhile, others have looked for ways to simplify testing methods. An example of this is SalivaDirect, which allows samples to be collected for PCR tests using saliva rather than a deep nasal swab.[30] The advantage of a saliva test is that it can be administered by non-professionals or even self-administered. Evidence suggests that the outcomes are similar.[31] As we will see in the next chapter, there are other types of tests that also reduce costs. However, are these tests sufficient for informing decisions about whether to isolate people? That is the critical question.

---

[29] Gideon Lewis-Kraus, "Jonathan Rothberg's Race to Invent the Ultimate Rapid At-Home Covi-19 Test," *The New Yorker*, August 29, 2020, https://www.newyorker.com/tech/annals-of-technology/jonathan-rothbergs-race-to-invent-the-ultimate-rapid-at-home-covid-19-test.

[30] Chantal B.F. Vogels, Anne E. Watkins, Christina A. Harden, Doug E. Brackney, Jared Shafer, Jianhui Wang, Cesar Caraballo et al, "SalivaDirect: A Simplified and Flexible Platform to Enhance SARS-CoV-2 Testing Capacity," *Med* (December 25, 2020), https://www.cell.com/med/fulltext/S2666-6340(20)30076-3.

[31] Andreas K. Lindner, Olga Nikolai, Chiara Rohardt, Franka Kausch, Mia Wintel, Maximilian Gertler, Susen Burock et al., "SARS-CoV-2 Patient Self-Testing with an Antigen-Detecting Rapid Test: A Head-to-Head Comparison with Professional Testing," *medRxiv* (January 2021).

Is It Really the Gold Standard?

Cost. When it comes down to it, all of the limitations related to using PCR tests to solve the pandemic information gap resolve into one thing: cost. Providing and processing tests are expensive efforts. The way in which samples are collected requires training health workers, and testing is uncomfortable for those being tested. These hurdles complicate our ability to deploy tests at scale. In countries where the pandemic has been most prevalent, access to tests has been, consequently, restricted.

What we get in return for this cost is "gold-standard quality." It's true that PCR tests can detect even the smallest traces of the coronavirus in individuals. Thus, medical professionals argue the following:

> The "gold standard" refers to the highest quality, or benchmark, of a specific practice, product or technology. . . . Other diagnostic testing methods, like culture or serology, may not provide the same level of sensitivity as PCR. Therefore, the risk of false negatives increases in critical testing scenarios where organisms or viruses may be difficult to grow, or detect an immune response to. This is why PCR is considered the gold standard by many across the diagnostic community.[32]

But do we really need tests that are able to do that? For a test to be the "gold-standard," it must tell us the information we need to make decisions without error. How do PCR tests score on that metric?

Before delving into that, let me abuse you with one notion: that "better" information leads to better decisions. Let's move away from tests for the moment and think of other ways we try and detect things. One way we can sniff out harmful stuff is to use sniffer dogs.

Just as astonishing, to Waggoner, is a dog's acuity—the way

---

[32] Roche, "What Is PCR and Why Is It the 'Gold Standard' in Molecular Diagnostics?", (May 1, 2020), https://diagnostics.roche.com/us/en/roche-blog/what-is-pcr-and-why-is-it-the--gold-standard--in-molecular-diagn.html.

it can isolate and identify compounds within a scent, like the spices in a soup. Drug smugglers often try to mask the smell of their shipments by packaging them with coffee beans, air fresheners, or sheets of fabric softener. To see if this can fool a dog, Waggoner has flooded his laboratory with different scents, then added minute quantities of heroin or cocaine to the mix. In one case, 'the whole damn lab smelled like a Starbucks,' he told me, but the dogs had no trouble homing in on the drug. 'They're just incredible at finding the needle in the haystack.'[33]

Dogs can be trained to seek out any chemical substance: stuff to make bombs, bed bugs, and (this will not surprise you), coronavirus carriers.[34] However, the chemicals that are specific to a particular thing might exist elsewhere.

Horacio Maldonado, one of the new recruits, positioned himself under an arched entrance on the west side of the station. His black Lab, Ray, could smell most of the passersby from there—she had a range of about thirty feet—but a crowd like this was full of false leads. The chemicals found in explosives can also be found in drugs, cosmetics, fertilizer, construction supplies, and other mundanities. I'd heard of a police dog driven wild by a table patched with plastic wood filler, and a dog tearing down a wall with nail-gun cartridges hidden inside it. 'I remember one time, we stopped a guy in Columbus Circle, he had two hundred nitrogen pills in his pocket,' Maldonado told me. 'Turned out he was going to Europe and had just come from his doctor. So you've got to use your common sense. The guy's sixty, seventy-years old. He isn't sweating. Does he look like a suicide bomber?'

As the dog cannot distinguish the chemical from its source or the

---

[33] Burkard Bilger, "Beware of the Dogs," *The New Yorker*, February 27, 2012.

[34] Susan Hazel and Anne-Lise Chaber, "These Dogs Are Trained to Sniff Out the Coronavirus. Most have a 100% Success Rate," (The Conversation, August 4, 2020), https://theconversation.com/these-dogs-are-trained-to-sniff-out-the-coronavirus-most-have-a-100-success-rate-143756.

amount of the chemical, there are false positives. This could be disruptive. If someone was moving an explosive around an airport in a bag, we would have to be concerned that a dog might end up targeting the wrong bags.

We are familiar with something being too sensitive. Do we want a fire alarm that is set to go off at the slightest hint of smoke? If not, do we need a fire alarm that is so good that it can detect the slightest hint of smoke?

Herein lies the issue with PCR tests. They can be too good. To be sure, if the coronavirus is present in a body, they will pick it up. But they cannot tell whether the coronavirus is active or inactive. When it is active, we care. When it is inactive, not so much. An inactive virus does not need antiviral treatment (that might have side effects). An inactive virus is not contagious, so we do not need to isolate the person.

Thus, even when diagnosing for treatment, the PCR test can be a bit much. From *The New York Times*:[35]

> One solution would be to adjust the cycle threshold used to decide that a patient is infected. Most tests set the limit at forty, a few at thirty-seven. This means that you are positive for the coronavirus if the test process required up to forty cycles, or thirty-seven, to detect the virus.
>
> Tests with thresholds so high may detect not just live virus but also genetic fragments, leftovers from infection that pose no particular risk—akin to finding a hair in a room long after a person has left, Dr. Mina said.
>
> Any test with a cycle threshold above thirty-five is too sensitive, agreed Juliet Morrison, a virologist at the University of California, Riverside. 'I'm shocked that people would think that forty could represent a positive,' she said.

---

[35] Apoorva Mandavilli, "Your Coronavirus Test Is Positive. Maybe It Shouldn't Be," *The New York Times,* August 29, 2020, https://www.nytimes.com/2020/08/29/health/coronavirus-testing.html.

A more reasonable cutoff would be thirty to thirty-five, she added. Dr. Mina said he would set the figure at thirty, or even less. Those changes would mean the amount of genetic material in a patient's sample would have to be a hundredfold to a thousandfold that of the current standard for the test to return a positive result.

In other words, even for doctors thinking about treatment, PCR tests detect smoke where there is no fire.

So, who is setting the dial on PCR test thresholds?

The Food and Drug Administration said in an emailed statement that it does not specify the cycle threshold ranges used to determine who is positive, and that 'commercial manufacturers and laboratories set their own.'

The Centers for Disease Control and Prevention said it is examining the use of cycle threshold measures 'for policy decisions.' The agency said it would need to collaborate with the FDA and with device manufacturers to ensure the measures 'can be used properly and with assurance that we know what they mean.'

The CDC's own calculations suggest that it is extremely difficult to detect any live virus in a sample above a threshold of thirty-three cycles. Officials at some state labs said the CDC had not asked them to note threshold values or to share them with contact-tracing organizations.

For example, North Carolina's state lab uses the Thermo Fisher coronavirus test, which automatically classifies results based on a cutoff of thirty-seven cycles. A spokeswoman for the lab said testers did not have access to the precise numbers.

Apparently, it is not clear. That is a problem given how much it can matter.

Figure 2.3: Viral Load, Diagnosis and Decisions

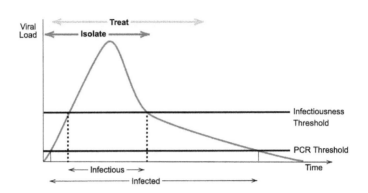

Figure 2.3 shows why this is an issue. It demonstrates the typical path of the viral load in someone with Covid-19, from the date he or she is infected to the time when the person is no longer infected. Notice that in the first day or so the viral load is small but growing quickly. Between days three and seven it grows many billions of times. The scale on the Y-axis of this figure is logarithmic (corresponding to the Ct score described earlier, with the PCR threshold set at Ct of forty and the infectiousness threshold at about a Ct above thirty). Thus, the difference between the peak and any other point is scaled down visually. At this point, there is maximal viral shedding; that is, the virus is present in such quantities that it can also leave the body in large quantities and infect others.[36] After it reaches a peak, the virus stops spreading in the body and starts to die. Notice, therefore, that if an asymptomatic patient had a PCR test at a random point in the cycle, with about two-thirds probability, that patient would test positive even though the virus

---

[36] Jeroen J.A. van Kampen, David AMC van de Vijver, Pieter LA Fraaij, Bart L. Haagmans, Mart M. Lamers, Nisreen Okba, Johannes PC van den Akker, et al., "Duration and Key Determinants of Infectious Virus Shedding in Hospitalized Patients with Coronavirus Disease (Covid-19)," *Nature Communications* 12, no. 1, (2019): 1-6.

detected would, in fact, be inactive.[37] Specifically, if a doctor knew this, he or she would not treat that patient for Covid-19 if the patient did not have symptoms. From a diagnostic perspective, absent other information, the PCR test would yield substantial false positives.

The fundamental problem here is not that PCR tests do not provide information about viral load—they do generate a Ct score that doctors can use to assess someone's stage in the cycle. If doctors take two PCR tests two days apart, they can see the change in the Ct score and, therefore, have a good sense of whether a patient is over the hump or not. Instead, the problem is that the Ct number is rarely reported to doctors at all. All that is reported is whether the coronavirus is detected according to the threshold set by the lab.

This is relevant because PCR tests have thresholds that are chosen; hence, it is possible to choose a different threshold and change the sensitivity and specificity of a test. This is well known.

> However, the problem with a Ct-based diagnosis is that there is no absolute or constant Ct cut-off value, and Ct cut-off values are different for each diagnostic reagent even for the same gene. For example, although there are differences according to diagnostic reagents, *a sample is usually judged positive for Covid-19 based on a Ct value of thirty-five* [emphasis added]. Although the Ct value in a rRT-PCR test is relatively accurate, errors of 1-2 cycles are not uncommon in a Ct value depending on various factors, including the skill of the examiner. Therefore, when there is ambiguity in the Ct value, such as thirty-four or thirty-six, the result may be interpreted as false negative or false positive depending on the Ct cut-off value.[38]

---

[37] Kaiyuan Sun, Wei Wang, Lidong Gao, Yan Wang, Kaiwei Luo, Lingshuang Ren, Zhifei Zhan, et al., "Transmission Heterogeneities, Kinetics, and Controllability of SARS-CoV-2," *Science* (2020).

[38] M.C. Chang, J. Hur, and D. Park, "Interpreting the Covid-19 Test Results: A Guide for Physiatrists," *American Journal of Physical Medicine and Rehabilitation* 99, no. 7, (2020): 583–585. https://doi.org/10.1097/PHM.0000000000001471.

The key phrase above is in italics. What we should know is that that level of Ct is a very low one, meaning that the PCR threshold is set so that a positive result can be returned even if there are very few coronavirus RNA remnants present in the solution. In other words, it is extremely specific. To come back negative, there really can't be *any* coronavirus remnants.

This raises an obvious question: Why is a threshold set at all? When performing a PCR test, the lab could actually report the Ct number. Then a doctor could judge what that means. Instead, thresholds are hard-wired into machines, and the machines only report whether outcomes are positive or negative. So, even if we knew the threshold for "negative" used by each machine/lab, the number for a positive result could be any number above that threshold.

> This amounts to an enormous, missed opportunity to learn more about the disease, some experts said.

> 'It's just kind of mind-blowing to me that people are not recording the Ct values from all these tests—that they're just returning a positive or a negative,' said Angela Rasmussen, a virologist at Columbia University in New York. 'It would be useful information to know if somebody's positive, whether they have a high viral load or a low viral load,' she added.

This really matters for interpretation.

> Officials at the Wadsworth Center, New York's state lab, have access to Ct values from tests they have processed, and analyzed their numbers at *The Times's* request. In July, the lab identified 794 positive tests, based on a threshold of forty cycles.

> With a cutoff of thirty-five, about half of those tests would no longer qualify as positive. About 70 percent would no longer be judged positive if the cycles were limited to thirty.

> In Massachusetts, from 85 to 90 percent of people who tested

positive in July with a cycle threshold of forty would have been deemed negative if the threshold were thirty cycles, Dr. Mina said. . . .

'I'm really shocked that it could be that high—the proportion of people with high Ct value results,' said Dr. Ashish Jha, director of the Harvard Global Health Institute. 'Boy, does it really change the way we need to be thinking about testing.'

Dr. Jha said he had thought of the PCR test as a problem because it cannot scale to the volume, frequency, or speed of tests needed. 'But what I am realizing is that a really substantial part of the problem is that we're not even testing the people who we need to be testing,' he said.

Those are big numbers. The reality is that we don't really know the real-time numbers about infectious people, and even if we used daily PCR tests on everyone we still wouldn't know.[39] We might eventually know those numbers, but without them now, we can't take action to mitigate historic pandemics!

Current practice is determined at the regulatory level, which often places restrictions on whether Ct numbers can be reported to doctors and patients alike.[40] For example, here is what Ontario Public Health says about this practice:

Some experts have argued that Ct values should be provided routinely on laboratory reports to assist with clinical and public health decision making. This may be applicable in a

[39] Michael R. Tom and Michael J. Mina, "To Interpret the SARS-CoV-2 Test, Consider the Cycle Threshold Value," *Clinical Infectious Diseases* 71, no. 16, (October 15, 2020): 2252–2254, https://doi.org/10.1093/cid/ciaa619.

[40] There has been regulatory uncertainty regarding this reporting. There are suggestions that the FDA never prohibited that reporting. See: Apoorva Mandavilli, "You're Infected with the Coronavirus. But How Infected?" *The New York Times,* December 29, 2020, https://www.nytimes.com/2020/12/29/health/coronavirus-viral-load.html. But, as of December 2020, the FDA has been more explicit regarding permitting labs to estimate a patient's viral load. Florida's Department of Health now requires this reporting. See: Florida Health, "Mandatory Reporting of COVID-19 Laboratory Test Results: Reporting of Cycle Threshold Values," (December 3, 2020), https://www.flhealthsource.gov/files/Laboratory-Reporting-CT-Values-12032020.pdf.

limited setting where healthcare providers only receive reports from a single laboratory, and can be educated about the test performance and Ct value characteristics of a particular assay. *However, in complex laboratory network environments, such as in Ontario, where specimens may be tested at one of several laboratories (> 40 laboratories conducting SARS-CoV-2 rRT-PCR in the province on a variety of different extraction and PCR platforms), utility of such reporting is questionable. Moreover, test results are received and reviewed by a myriad of healthcare providers, as well as patients, with varying understanding of Ct values* [emphasis added]. As such, the inclusion of Ct values on laboratory reports issued in Ontario (and Canada) is not recommended—they are of limited utility if used in isolation when interpreting the rRT-PCR result. In the rare, specific scenarios where it is thought that the Ct value might inform clinical or public health management, clinical and public health providers should contact the testing laboratory to discuss Ct interpretation, in the context of the epidemiology and clinical scenario, with the microbiology team.[41]

Suffice it to say, this rationale is far from clear. The argument for providing Ct scores is that they will inform us when making critical decisions. The argument against them seems to be that doctors might rely on them to make decisions! Thus, false positives are baked into PCR tests by design.

Seen this way, it is not that PCR tests do not have better information than other methods. They do. But these tests are used in a way that throws important information away, which means that the actual reports are less informative. That reduction in informativeness increases the potential for errors in decisions that rely on the reported PCR results. It makes them like oversensitive bomb sniffing dogs, which means that decision-makers must make

---

[41] Public Health Ontario, "An Overview of Cycle Threshold Values and their Role in SARS-CoV-2 Real-Time PCR Test Interpretation," (September 17, 2020), https://www.publichealthontario.ca/-/media/documents/ncov/main/2020/09/cycle-threshold-values-sars-cov2-pcr.pdf.

adjustments to deal with the uncertainty.

Infection Versus Infectiousness

These issues become even more problematic when we consider the other role of PCR tests: informing decisions about whether to isolate people.

Consider again figure 2.3. That graph shows the difference between being infected (as reported by a PCR test) and being infectious (able to spread the coronavirus). To be infectious, a person must be infected, but the converse does not hold. If we only want to isolate people who are infectious, then a choice to isolate all infected people would lead us to isolate too many people. That choice adds costs, notably to the isolated people. There are also other consequences. In chapter 4, we will look at contact tracing whereby the close contacts of an infectious person are identified and isolated. However, if someone is infected and not infectious, those egregious measures would be pointless, even though the costs would be multiplied.

There are significant costs associated with the alternative, to not isolate an infectious person. Thus, we want to be cautious in our assessment of whether someone is infectious. Caution leads us to set the infectiousness threshold (used to determine whether to isolate someone) lower than might be required if we had all of the information at hand. If we were looking at Ct scores for this purpose, we would set a higher Ct score as the threshold. At the time of this writing, it is believed that a conservative threshold would be a viral load of 10^6 copies per million.[42] This is many orders of magnitude higher than the threshold for a typical PCR test of 10^3 copies per

---

[42] Larremore, Daniel B., Bryan Wilder, Evan Lester, Soraya Shehata, James M. Burke, James A. Hay, Milind Tambe, Michael J. Mina, and Roy Parker. "Test sensitivity is secondary to frequency and turnaround time for COVID-19 screening." *Science Advances* (2020): eabd5393.

million.

The point is this: Because we do not look at Ct scores and simply isolate infected people, we are potentially isolating too many people, even as we minimize the risk of not isolating infectious individuals.

Antigen Tests

PCR tests are not the only game in town. The other major type of tests for the coronavirus are antigen tests. These tests are significantly cheaper and they can provide rapid results. Here I will set those advantages aside and consider antigen tests in terms of how they assist in decisions about whether to isolate someone. In other words, I will address this question: How useful are antigen tests in solving the fundamental pandemic information gap?

Whereas a PCR test looks for the genetic markers of a virus, antigen tests look for the proteins associated with cells that have been infected by the virus. Also, the way in which antigen tests are processed means that the threshold above which they detect the virus's presence is higher than the PCR test. For a typical antigen test, it is at 10^5 copies per million or higher. Figure 2.4 shows the difference.

As you move from the PCR to the antigen threshold, there are two impacts on a decision to isolate. We want to isolate someone as soon as he or she is infected, but only until the virus crosses the infectiousness threshold (10^3 copies per million, or a Ct of about thirty). At that point, the antigen test provides a better indicator than a PCR test of whether to release someone from isolation. One or two negative PCR tests are usually required for such releases, but we can see that the equivalent number of antigen tests would lead to better release decisions.

Figure 2.4: Viral Load and Antigen Tests

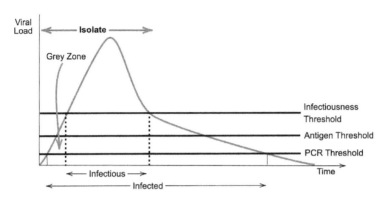

The same is true for decisions to isolate. Remember, we want to isolate a person soon after he or she is infected, before the viral load reaches the infectiousness threshold. If we had results at the time a test is performed, both the PCR and the antigen tests would fulfill that requirement.[43] Thus, because the antigen threshold lies below the infectiousness threshold, moving from a PCR test to an antigen test does not increase the risk of releasing an infectious person. Conversely, what *does* change is the risk of isolating someone who is not infectious. This risk is reduced significantly by using an antigen test compared to using a PCR test.

Nonetheless, there is a grey zone (as depicted in figure 2.4). At this point, we might want to isolate a person because he or she will *soon become infectious.* There is a moment when the PCR test will detect a prospective infectious person whereas an antigen test might miss that person. In the next chapter, I argue, however, that because PCR test results are often delayed, that advantage is diminished. Moreover, because antigen tests can be conducted more frequently, that risk is mitigated; missed infectious people will be picked up on

---

[43] If there is a delay in results, this becomes an issue. Something discussed in detail in chapter 3.

a subsequent screen.

This demonstrates that an antigen test is actually more informative—in the sense of leading to better decisions—for the decision of whether to isolate someone when compared with the "gold-standard" PCR test.[44] Antigen tests are more likely to be associated with the viral load of an infectious person than PCR tests (or at least those PCR tests that don't include a Ct score report).[45]

Clinical evaluations of antigen tests by regulators confirm these advantages, even in contests that are stacked against antigen tests.[46] When Abbott submitted its BinaxNOW test to the Food and Drug Administration (FDA) for emergency use authorization, the accompanying study showed that, compared with a PCR test, there was a positive agreement of thirty-four out of thirty-five PCR test-positive subjects (or 97.1 percent) and a negative agreement of sixty-six out of sixty-seven PCR test negative subjects (or 98.5 percent).[47] That said, this was a small sample, so the FDA assessed that the sensitivity of the BinaxNOW test for infection was likely between 85 and 99 percent. The FDA only cared about the accuracy of the BinaxNOW test for infection.

However, the Abbott study produced some interesting results about infectiousness. The PCR results included the Ct score for the study. If we compare the agreement for Ct scores below thirty-

---

[44] What all this means is that, apart from anything else, we should dial down those thresholds on PCR tests. We likely need high thresholds for treatment, but we probably need to dial down thresholds further when testing for infectiousness. Either that, or we should report the Ct number so that those who use the test can match that information with the purpose at hand.

[45] Joshua S. Gans, "Test Sensitivity for Infection Versus Infectiousness of SARS-CoV-2," medRxiv (2020).

[46] Covid, UK, Lateral Flow Oversight Team, and Tim Peto, "Covid-19: Rapid Antigen detection for SARS-CoV-2 by Lateral Flow Assay: A National Systematic Evaluation for Mass-Testing," medRxiv, (January 2021); Eliseo Albert, Ignacio Torres, Felipe Bueno, et al., "Field Evaluation of a Rapid Antigen Test . . . for Covid-19 Diagnosis in Primary Healthcare Centers," Clinical Microbiology and Infection (2020); and I.W. Pray, L. Ford, D. Cole, et al., "Performance of an Antigen-Based Test for Asymptomatic and Symptomatic SARS-CoV-2 Testing at Two University Campuses—Wisconsin, MMWR Morb Mortal Weekly Report 69 (2020):1642–1647.

[47] Food and Drug Administration, Abbott Procedure Card, (December 2020), https://www.fda.gov/media/141570/download.

three (a higher viral load), then there are no false negatives. In other words, the one infected person that the Abbott test missed had a low viral load (a Ct score above thirty-three). Similar results have been confirmed again and again. For high viral loads, antigen test sensitivity is virtually identical to PCR tests.[48]

---

[48] Pekosz, Andrew, Charles Cooper, Valentin Parvu, et al., "Antigen-Based Testing but not Real-Time PCR Correlates with SARS-CoV-2 Virus Culture," *medRxiv* (2020); Eliseo Albert, et al., "Field Evaluation," (2020); Kerri Basile, Kenneth McPhie, Ian Carter, "Cell-Based Culture of SARS-CoV-2 Informs Infectivity and Safe Deisolation Assessments During Covid-19," *medRxiv* (2020); Hendrik Gremmels, Beatrice M.F. Winkel, Rob Schuurman, et al., "Real-Life Validation of the Panbio™ Covid-19 Antigen Rapid Test (Abbott) in Community-Dwelling Subjects with Symptoms of Potential SARS-CoV-2 Infection," *EClinicalMedicine* (2020): 100677.

3
Screening for Safety

Current testing systems were built to identify infected people and treat them. They could also inform decisions about isolation. Unfortunately, the fundamental pandemic information gap arises because we choose to be, in many respects, cautious with respect to our prediction that any one person might be infectious. When we are cautious, we treat many more people as infectious and then isolate them. This would be less needed if we had accurate predictions about potentially infectious individuals. The consequences of social distancing or isolation, which both rest on beliefs that the average person is more infectious than we know, include reductions in economic activity and other social losses. The key to mitigating these losses is to provide ways to plug the information gap.

Absent diagnostic tests, the main way we distinguish between people in terms of their risk of infectiousness is via a screening process. To date, the primary methods by which people are screened is through an assessment of whether they have Covid-19 symptoms, have had contact with infected people recently, or have engaged in other risky behavior (such as travel to high prevalence locations). The idea is that if a person "passes" a screen, he or she can enter a location, and if a person does not pass the screen, the individual cannot enter. In some cases, other things might happen, including quarantine and follow-up examinations. In this way, by screening people according to the risk of infectiousness, others can be protected.

The antigen tests discussed in the previous chapter have the potential to be an important part of a screening system. They are cheaper than PCR tests (less than $10 rather than $60 or more), and they yield results quickly (in five to thirty minutes compared with eight hours or longer). The distinction is important because infectiousness is something that is detected at the time a test is taken and, as will be explained, delays reduce the usefulness of a test as a screen.

From this perspective, when screening is the objective, it is perhaps better to refer to antigen tools as *screens* rather than tests. In fact, from now on I will refer to them as antigen screens for this reason. Thus, rather than evaluate whether they correlate with known measures of Covid-19 infection, we will evaluate how well they help us assess the risk of an individual's infectiousness to others. If the goal of a screen is to clear people for various activities, then the efficacy of the screen is measured by how informative they are in providing a prediction of individual riskiness.

Evaluating Riskiness

To begin, it is important to have a clearer understanding of the criteria we need in order to best evaluate whether someone is more or less risky to interact with others. These criteria can be applied to antigen screens, and to symptoms and other indicators of infectiousness.

To build intuition, suppose we had a perfect screen. In this case, if a person passed the screen, we would know with 100 percent certainty that he or she was not infectious with Covid-19, and if the person did not pass the screen, we would know with 100 percent certainty that he or she was infectious. In that situation, following a positive screen result, we would assess the individual as being infectious with 100 percent probability and, following a negative screen result, we would assess that person as being infectious with 0 percent probability. The decision as to whether to isolate the person from others would be straightforward.

Our evaluation becomes more difficult when the screen is imperfect. Two issues arise. First, we need to distinguish between the probability that someone was infectious prior to being screened and how that probability is adjusted based on the result of the screen. In other words, when screens are imperfect, the post-screen probability that someone is infectious depends on the pre-screen probability. Second, because it is possible to have false-positive and false-negative screens, we need to consider the consequences and costs associated with errors. If screens were perfect, we would not have to worry about the consequences of errors. With imperfect screens, possible errors become a consideration, especially when determining the thresholds by which a screen might impact a clearance decision.

With respect to screening during a pandemic, the cost of errors tends to be considered as one-sided. There is a very high cost of erroneously admitting an infectious person into a location because he or she might infect others. By contrast, the choice to turn the individual away, given that there is already a high degree of social distancing, is relatively less costly. Thus, with respect to clearance, we tend to worry more about false negatives than false positives. That said, from an individual perspective, the private costs of false positives are potentially quite high. As we will discuss below, the fear of personal costs might cause people to be more reluctant to submit to screening procedures.

Figure 3.1: Pre- and Post-Screen Probabilities

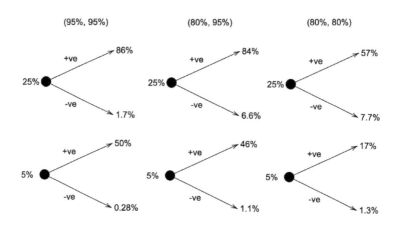

A Tale of Two Probabilities

Let's turn to our assessment of the likelihood of whether someone is infectious based on that person's pre-screen probability and the error rates associated with a screen.

Figure 3.1 shows the pre- and post-screen probabilities for different sensitivities (the first bracketed number) and specificities (the second bracketed number).[49] For instance, in the first panel, sensitivity and specificity are both 95 percent, meaning that there is a 5 percent probability of a false negative and a 5 percent probability of a false positive. In that situation, if the screen is applied to an individual with a 25 percent pre-screen probability of being infectious, then a positive screen result would raise that probability to 86 percent and a negative screen result would lower it to 1.7 percent. By contrast, the same screen applied to an individual

---

[49] The formula for these calculations is based on Bayes Rule. Suppose that p is the pre-screen probability, and that sensitivity is x and specificity is y. Then the post-screen probability, if there is a positive screen result, is $px/(px + (1-p)(1-y))$. If there is a negative screen result, it is $(1-p)y/(p(1-x) + (1-p)y)$. Thus, if $x = y = 0.95$ and $p = 0.25$, then these probabilities are approximately 0.86 and 0.017, respectively.

with a 5 percent pre-screen probability of being infectious increases to a 50 percent probability following a positive screen result and falls to 0.28 percent following a negative one. We can see that as pre-screen probability falls, so too falls the probability that a person is infectious.

By contrast, a change in the error rate of a screen reduces the gap between the post-screen probabilities—that is, our ability to distinguish between infectious and noninfectious individuals. A fall in sensitivity (i.e., an increase in false negatives) reduces our ability to infer that a person is not infectious. A fall in specificity (i.e., an increase in false positives) reduces our ability to infer that a person is infectious. Notice that when the pre-screen probability that someone is infectious is low, then a screen with a lower sensitivity and specificity, while offering some information, does not offer a clear picture of who is infectious and who is not infectious. Any decision made in that context has a high probability of being in error.

Are Temperature Checks Good Screens?

We can use this framework to evaluate any information we might use as a screen. As with other symptom checks, identifying a fever is sometimes used as a screen for Covid-19. Many people who have Covid-19 with symptoms also present a high temperature. Moreover, the timing of a fever often overlaps with the time someone might be infectious (rather than just infected).

Temperature checks have been widely used during the Covid-19 pandemic. Some places—such as doctors' offices—conduct them on entry. More often, as part of the school or work protocol, people are asked to check their temperatures at home and to certify they do not have a fever. No one disagrees that having a fever is highly indicative of Covid-19 infection. But the question is:

Can temperature checks help?

Some have raised doubts.

> But experts and medical groups increasingly say that isn't
> a good gauge of Covid-19 as many infected children and
> adults don't get fevers. Furthermore, variability in individual
> temperatures as well as questions about the accuracy of body-
> temperature scanners and infrared contact-free thermometers
> put such checks at risk of potential error.[50]

There is potentially a litany of issues with obsessive temperature checking, including the accuracy of thermometers and the possibility of fevers being caused by factors other than Covid-19.

What does the data say about this question? The CDC studied three hundred children with Covid-19 and found that 56 percent had a fever. This is a calculation of the sensitivity of temperature as a signal of Covid-19; that is, the percentage of people with fevers who are truly positive for Covid-19. However, the calculation does not tell us the specificity of temperature checks; that is, the percentage of people with fevers who do not have Covid-19. Some people will fall into this group because fevers are caused by many things other than Covid-19. Nonetheless, if we assume that only a few kids are likely to have a fever caused by non-Covid-19 factors (say, a specificity of 95 percent), then if a child had a fever and the overall rate of Covid-19 among children was 1 percent, then the probability that the child has Covid-19 would be 10 percent. That is more than twenty times the probability of someone who does not have a fever. That is a significant indicator of a problem. I would hope that we would not allow people who have a one-in-ten chance of having Covid-19 into schools.

What about adults? The most comprehensive study examined

---

[50] Sumathi Reddy, "Temperature Isn't a Good Litmus Test for Coronavirus, Doctors Say," *The Wall Street Journal*, September 21, 2020, https://www.wsj.com/articles/temperature-isnt-a-good-litmus-test-for-coronavirus-doctors-say-11600713159.

Swiss military personnel.[51] Researchers studied eighty-four Covid-positive people and took their temperatures daily over a period of fourteen days. Covid-19 patients did have fevers, especially between two and six days after diagnosis. But if we used 38°C as the threshold for designating a person's temperature as a fever, only 18 percent of the patients would have a fever for some period of time. Drop that threshold to 37.1°C and the percentage increases to 63 percent. Why not just use that lower threshold? In that case, the number of false positives rises significantly with the specificity of the temperature check falling from 99 percent to 95 percent.

What does this mean? Figure 3.2 shows some examples. If we use a 38°C threshold (with 99 percent specificity and 1 percent prevalence), then a fever would indicate a 15 percent probability that an individual has Covid-19. However, the potential for errors is large, with few people being identified by this method and a small number of both false positives and false negatives. With a 38°C threshold (with 95 percent specificity and 1 percent prevalence), a

Figure 3.2: Pre- and Post-Screen Probabilities (Temperature)

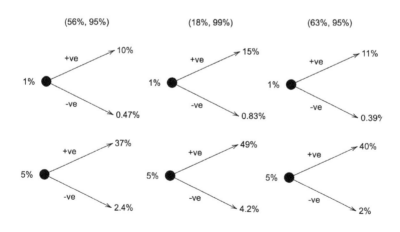

[51] M. Bielecki, G. Crameri, P. Schlagenhauf, T.W. Buehrer, and J.W. Deuel, Body Temperature Screening to Identify SARS-CoV-2 Infected Young Adult Travellers Is Ineffective," *Travel Medicine and Infectious Disease 37*, (September-October 2020), https://doi.org/10.1016/j.tmaid.2020.101832; https://www.ncbi.nlm.nih.gov/pmc/articles/PMC7403846.

fever would indicate an 11 percent probability that an individual has Covid-19. We would likely detect Covid-19 in some people without false negatives, but false positives would be very high (5 percent of the population). If the prevalence of Covid-19 in the population rises, the usefulness of temperature checks really goes up. With 5 percent prevalence, a fever would indicate that an individual has Covid-19 with more than 40 percent probability.

This all suggests to me that temperature checks are far from useless, but we have to be cautious about the presence of fevers. As before, temperature checks become more useful when background prevalence of Covid-19 is higher.

Antigen Screens As Pre-Screens

The value of screening is that it changes the risk assessment of an individual. Below we will continue to explore how screening impacts clearance and isolation decisions. Given the discussion above, it is useful to reflect on how antigen screens might assist in solving one of the big issues associated with testing in general: PCR tests are expensive and in limited supply. Can antigen screens help us economize on PCR test use?

Figure 3.3: Pre- and Post-Screen Probabilities (PCR Test)

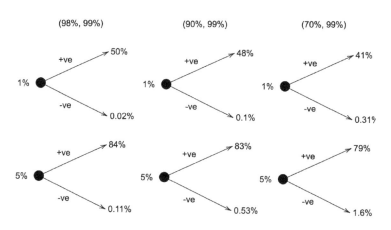

Figure 3.3 shows the pre- and post-screen probabilities of receiving a PCR test. Such tests have high specificity (here listed as 99 percent), but they vary in their sensitivity due mostly to variations in the field. The range presented corresponds to ranges observed in field evaluations of PCR test results.[52] Thus, we can see that when there is relatively low prevalence in the population, even a positive PCR test may only indicate a fifty-fifty chance that an individual has Covid-19. This is why PCR tests are usually only conducted when there are reasons for an individual's pre-test probability to be high, such as symptoms or exposure to a known case.

---

[52] Steven Woloshin, Neeraj Patel, and Aaron S. Kesselheim, "False Negative Tests for SARS-CoV-2 Infection—Challenges and Implications," *New England Journal of Medicine* (2020).

Figure 3.4: Combination Antigen and PCR

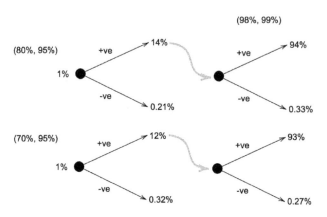

However, an antigen screen could also serve to change the pre-test probability for a PCR test. Some examples are provided in figure 3.4. There, two different antigen screens differing in sensitivity for infection (80 percent and 70 percent, respectively) are used on asymptomatic people from a population within which prevalence is 1 percent. Recall that in this situation, a positive, highly sensitive (98 percent) PCR test alone would indicate that an individual had Covid-19 with a 50 percent probability (figure 3.3). If that PCR test is conducted following a positive antigen result, those probabilities would rise to 93 to 94 percent even with antigen screens with very different error rates.[53]

Consider what this means for the cost of conducting overall testing. If we had one hundred people, we could run PCR tests on them all for approximately $10,000 (assuming an average cost of $100). For that, we would find one person who was positive, but we would also misidentify another person as positive. By contrast, if we run antigen screens on those one hundred people first, then we would, using the less sensitive screen, identify three people who are

---

[53] This result is proven formally by Jeffrey Ely, Andrea Galeotti, and Jakub Steiner, "*Optimal Test Allocation*," (Mimeo, Northwestern, 2020).

positive and only one who is truly positive. The total cost, therefore, of identifying the needle in the haystack (i.e., the one person who is positive given prevalence levels) is $1,000 (assuming an average antigen screen cost of $10) plus $300 (for three confirmatory PCR tests). Thus, not only would we reduce costs significantly, we would also increase the overall accuracy compared to solely relying on PCR tests.

In summary, even if we are wedded to the view that PCR tests are the gold standard for identifying people infected with Covid-19, using antigen screens can reduce costs and improve the accuracy of PCR tests.

Rapid Results

Cost, however, is only one part of achieving the scale necessary for successful mitigation. The other facet is speed—how quickly results can be provided after someone has been tested. Figure 3.5 demonstrates why that matters. If someone received a PCR test in the "grey zone" on day two (point A) and it took between a day (points B, C, D) and a week for results to be received, then that person would either be isolated needlessly or not isolated soon enough. We can compare those outcomes with someone who

Figure 3.5: Test Turnaround Time

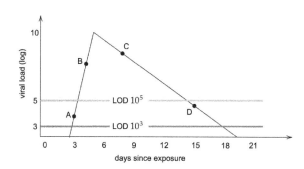

received an antigen screen and an immediate result on day 3 (point B).[54] This delay is the reason Bill Gates regarded most tests in the US as "garbage."

Interestingly, the same methods we use to produce lower-cost screens can also speed up the process. Speed increases as we reduce reliance on labs and machines, which are themselves major cost components of PCR tests. However, the main benefit of screening someone who is infectious is that he or she can be immediately isolated. The alternative is to require everyone tested to be isolated until the results are available. This, however, is costly, especially if there is no reason to suspect that someone has Covid-19 (i.e., the person's pre-test probability is low). That approach can also cause people to avoid testing because they know they will be immediately isolated.

Frequent Screening

Lower costs allow us to test people more frequently. By doing this, we can potentially screen more people during the time they are infectious. This is a key part of any screening strategy designed to keep people safe. The goal is to break chains of transmission.

Let me refresh your memory about how epidemiologists often refer to the virulence of a virus. They use a number called the "basic reproduction number," or R, which is a measure of how many people on average a person who is infected with the virus will infect. One of the key drivers of R is how easily a virus is shed from an infectious person to another person. Infection might occur when people breathe aerosols or when droplets on surfaces are, for

---

[54] Daniel B. Larremore, Bryan Wilder, Evan Lester, Soraya Shehata, James M. Burke, James A. Hay, Milind Tambe, Michael J. Mina, and Roy Parker, "Test Sensitivity Is Secondary to Frequency and Turnaround Time for Covid-19 Screening," *Science Advances* (2020): eabd5393.

example, transferred from hands to eyes. Both forms of transmission can be enhanced when people have symptoms such as coughing, but they are also mitigated by factors such as ventilation, wearing protective gear, and cleaning.

The other key driver of R is behavioral. Put simply, if infectious people are kept from being near others, R will be lower. Thus, R is driven by how many people are exposed to an infectious person while that person is infectious. Thus, if a person is infectious for five days, and if the period during which they interact with others is reduced to two or three of those days, R will be correspondingly halved. For the coronavirus, R was initially between two and three. More recently, R has been between 0.9 and 1.2 because in most places people have protected themselves and practiced social distancing.

If people are screened frequently, then the total duration of exposure can be limited. As a counterpoint, if people are screened twice daily, they could be isolated as soon as they become infectious, resulting in very short exposure times. Even if a person still manages to infect someone else, frequent screening could break the chain of transmission. We primarily care about reducing exposure, and that goal is affected by the frequency of screens and the accuracy of the screens. More frequent screening is good because infectious people can be identified and isolated quickly. More accurate screens are good because we are less likely to miss infectious people who would otherwise continue to do harm.

Thankfully, we do not need to dramatically increase the frequency of screening to have a large effect. Economists and epidemiologists have calculated the trade-offs involved.[55] The key threshold is how often we need to screen a population to get R below 1. If R falls below 1, we can wipe out the virus because each infected person will not spread the infection to another person (on average) and the growth rate of the outbreak will become negative.

---

[55] Ted Bergstrom, Carl T. Bergstrom, and Haoran Li, "Frequency and Accuracy of Proactive Testing for Covid-19," *medRxiv* (2020).

Figure 3.6: Estimated R

One Day Delay	Error rate				
	0.1	0.2	0.3	0.4	0.5
1 day	0.57	0.61	0.67	0.75	0.85
2 days	0.77	0.86	0.96	1.09	1.24
3.5 days	1.06	1.18	1.31	1.45	1.6
7 days	1.57	1.68	1.78	1.88	1.99

No Delay	Error rate				
	0.1	0.2	0.3	0.4	0.5
1 day	0.22	0.26	0.33	0.41	0.51
2 days	0.43	0.52	0.63	0.77	0.93
3.5 days	0.73	0.86	1.01	1.17	1.35
7 days	1.29	1.42	1.56	1.69	1.82

Source: Bergstrom, Bergstrom and Li (2020, Tables 2 and 6).
Calculations are for an R = 2.5.

Figure 3.6 shows the calculations depending on whether test results are returned in a day or without any delay. First assume that screen results arrive after a day and people are not isolated during that time. Then consider what happens if we screen every week and the error rate (for both false positives and false negatives) is 20 percent. In this scenario, R would fall to 1.68 from the baseline of 2.5. Next, if we increase the screening frequency to every two days, and the error rate remains at 20 percent, R would fall below 1 to 0.86. The situation improves even more if we obtain screen results without delay. In that case, and if the error rate remains at 20 percent, R would be 1.42 if we tested weekly and 0.52 if we tested every two days.

The figure above is helpful for determining screening frequencies, especially in environments where R would otherwise be high (e.g., a workplace where social distancing is impractical). The blue shaded regions show the frequency required to reduce the probability of an outbreak to a minimal level. Importantly, it also shows how to compensate for concerns about screening accuracy by screening more frequently.

In many places, the conditions required to prevent outbreaks are likely to be more favorable than those depicted in figure 3.6, where the assumed baseline R is 2.5. As noted, people are being cautious in many places, thereby moving R closer to 1. If, for example, $R = 1.2$ and there is a 30 percent error rate, we can get the effective R below 1 with a testing frequency of ten days.[56] In other words, screening once a week will be sufficient in many locations.

The University of Illinois

In the fall of 2020, many colleges across the US decided to bring students back to campus. There were real concerns that, students being students, outbreaks would occur on the campuses, possibly forcing closures and impacting nearby communities. To counter this, many campuses opted for systems of frequent screening.

The University of Illinois was a case in point. This campus has some forty thousand students with an additional six thousand staff. The university opened in August 2020 and immediately had a Covid-19 outbreak. This was of interest because university officials had invested in and adopted a practice of testing everyone frequently. Here are the details of their operation.

> Once the university had a viable test, the team had to determine how often to use it, how to notify people of the results, and then have a plan to isolate those who tested positive. "Fast and frequent" is the unofficial motto for the university's testing strategy.

> 'It really has to be that integrated, fast and frequent testing program to make the whole thing work,' Burke said. 'Because the pace at which the virus expands inside a person, you really do have a preciously short window of time to find out who's positive, quickly help them isolate safely and stop them from spreading it to others.'

---

[56] For a calculator see: https://steveli.shinyapps.io/FrequencyAndAccuracyCalculator.

Initially, the school thought they'd test once a week, but based on modeling, realized that twice a week would be most effective.

At nearly twenty testing sites set up across campus, students and staff can walk up and self-administer a free Covid-19 test. They are advised to avoid eating, drinking, brushing their teeth, chewing gum or smoking an hour before submitting their sample. Swiping their school ID prints a barcoded sticker that goes on their testing tube. They dribble half a teaspoon of saliva into the tube and put it on a rack with other samples. The whole process takes about seven minutes, Burke said.

Every hour, the racks of samples are delivered by golf cart to the campus' veterinary lab and go straight into the hot water bath to deactivate the virus. The lab runs tests 24 hours a day on weekdays, and nearly that on weekends.

When the lab scans the barcode on the test tube, it connects to the person's medical record. The results of the test are delivered via a HIPAA-compliant secure portal or app, dubbed Safer Illinois, that UIUC created. App users can also opt in to a Bluetooth feature that alerts them if they've spent more than fifteen minutes within six feet of a confirmed case and should get tested.

If faculty, staff and students receive a negative result at least every four days, they get a checkmark in the app and can enter campus buildings with their school ID. Some bars and restaurants are also using the app to let students gain entry, Burke said.

Another key feature of the school's Covid-19 strategy is isolating those who have tested positive as soon as possible. The university has found that the local health department has had trouble getting ahold of students promptly, with some students purposely ignoring the calls, Burke said, so it recently started directly reaching out to them. Its goal is to contact a positive case within thirty minutes and connect them with support.[57]

In other words, this was a serious and well-designed approach. So, what happened?

Almost everything in the plan worked as anticipated. University officials expected that students would gather at parties. And, in fact, the students partied.[58] As we have just shown, even when there is little social distancing, frequent screening can prevent outbreaks. So, the university did, in fact, conduct frequent tests. As of the end of 2020, the university had conducted over one million tests, corresponding to about 15 to 20 percent of all tests done in the state. The testing generally occurred twice per week. They used PCR tests with saliva samples processed on campus. Results were typically available within eight hours.

The problem was that, initially, administrators assumed that students who tested positive would self-isolate and not go to parties. That turned out to be a bad presumption. The administrators learned from this error.

Figure 3.7 shows the data. There was an outbreak about two weeks after students returned to campus. University officials quickly dealt with the outbreak via a two-week lockdown. Because testing was frequent, the detrimental behavior (going to parties while infectious) was quickly identified. The scale of the outbreak was known. The university dealt with the problem. Now there is a "normal" flow of cases with no further outbreaks.

---

[57] Meredith Deliso and Jay Bhatt, "Inside University of Illinois' Massive Covid-19 Testing Operation," (ABC News, September 10, 2020), https://abcnews.go.com/US/inside-university-illinois-massive-covid-19-testing-operation/story?id=72686799.

[58] Kenneth Chang, "A University Had a Great Coronavirus Plan, but Students Partied On," *The New York Times,* September 10, 2020, https://www.nytimes.com/2020/09/10/health/university-illinois-covid.html.

Figure 3.7: University of Illinois Cases and Testing (August-December 2020)

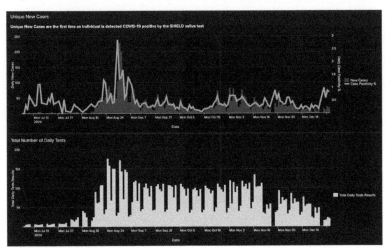

Source: Screenshot of https://go.illinois.edu/COVIDTestingData from December 30, 2020.

What this shows is that screening can work to make a place safe. It can work in an environment where people might be otherwise prone to engage in risky behavior. And it can be sustained. This raises the issue of whether a scaled and sustainable system can be built in other places—an issue that I take up in the next chapter.

4
Sustainable Systems

In October and November 2020, when faced with a rapidly increasing outbreak of Covid-19, Slovakia tried something new: It moved to test most of its population twice over a two-week period. There was a pilot effort in four regions of the country in October. The pilot had its bumps, but it turned out to be successful, with almost 141,000 of the estimated 155,000 eligible people being tested. They found 5,594 positive cases.

Following the pilot, the government conducted a first round of 3.4 million tests on the weekend of October 31 to November 1. The second round of testing came a week later with two million more tests. From *The Lancet:*

> For the mass testing, thousands of testing sites are to be set up across the country and everyone over the age of ten years—approximately four million people—will be asked to attend a testing site and take an antigen test. After being tested, people must wait in a separate disinfected room and, around half an hour later, will be given their results.[59]

This was the first time an entire country had opted to use antigen

[59] Edward Holt, "Slovakia to Test All Adults for SARS-CoV-2," *The Lancet* 396, no. 10260 (2020):1386-1387, https://www.thelancet.com/journals/lancet/article/PIIS0140-6736(20)32261-3/fulltext.

screens at this scale. If a person tested positive, he or she was required to stay home for ten days or go to a government quarantine site. Failure to do so attracted large fines. Getting a screen was voluntary; however, if a person did not complete a screen and have documentation to prove it, the government would restrict that individual's activities. Health officials were supported by the army to distribute and administer the tests.

The initial results were very favorable. Before the push, Slovakia had been identifying about twenty-five hundred cases per day. On that first weekend alone, they found thirty-eight thousand more. These were cases that would have otherwise been missed and also ones that were identified earlier. Either way, isolating infected people would help break chains of transmission. Another 13,500 people with Covid-19 were found in the second round. During the two weekends, the Slovakian outbreak peaked and then began to fall rapidly.[60] Slovakia reached its reopening target soon after and the government eased restrictions.[61]

The benefits turned out to be short-lived. When the screening stopped, the cases surged again. Figure 4.1 shows the roller-coaster ride. In the end, the program may have slowed the outbreak, but the positive outcome was temporary.[62] The program did not alleviate continuing pressure on the health care system or prevent further lockdowns.

Slovakia's hope for a good outcome might have been based, in part, on the successful mass testing program instituted by Wuhan,

---

[60] Mahase Elisabeth, "Covid-19: Mass Testing in Slovakia May Have Helped Cut Infections," BMJ 2020; 371 :m4761; M. Pavelka, K. van-Zandvoort, S. Abbott, et al., "The Effectiveness of Population-Wide, Rapid Antigen Test Based Screening in Reducing SARS-CoV-2 Infection Prevalence in Slovakia," *medRxiv* (2020), doi:10.1101/2020.12.02.20240648.

[61] Jason Hovet, "Slovakia to Ease Covid curbs As It Hails Mass Testing Success," *National Post*, November 13, 2020, https://nationalpost.com/pmn/entertainment-pmn/slovakia-to-ease-covid-curbs-as-it-hails-mass-testing-success.

[62] Edward Holt, "Covid-19 Testing in Slovakia," *The Lancet. Infectious Diseases* 21, no. 1, (2021): 32, https://www.thelancet.com/journals/laninf/article/PIIS1473-3099(20)30948-8/fulltext.

China in May 2020.[63] In that case, 9.9 million people received PCR tests in just over two weeks. The Chinese saw that testing effort as a critical step toward reopening the city in China hardest hit by Covid-19. They found three hundred infections. Shortly after, restrictions were lifted and life in Wuhan appeared to return to normal.

There was, however, a critical difference between Wuhan and Slovakia: the overall prevalence of Covid-19. Wuhan undertook its testing months into a strict lockdown during which most people stayed home. This meant that prevalence was extremely low. The mass testing put the icing on the cake by finding those few remaining infections and thereby enabling the city to reopen. In that respect, the prevailing conditions were similar to those faced by South Korea.

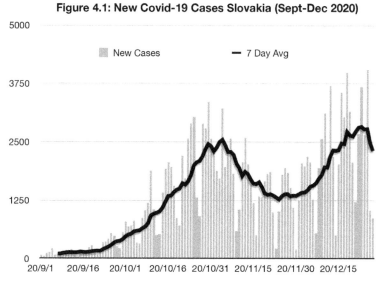

Figure 4.1: New Covid-19 Cases Slovakia (Sept-Dec 2020)

Source: ourworldindata.org (https://github.com/owid/covid-19-data/tree/master/public/data); accessed December 28, 2020

[63] Benjamin Fearnow, "Wuhan Tested Nearly 7 Million People in 12 Days to Prevent Second Coronavirus Wave, Health Officials Say," *Newsweek*, May 26, 2020, https://www.newsweek.com/wuhan-tested-nearly-7-million-people-12-days-prevent-second-coronavirus-wave-health-officials-say-1506537.

By contrast, Slovakia's testing occurred during the upswing of its strongest outbreak. There were restrictions in place but not to the same extent as China's. The mass screening was seen as a way of flattening the curve and as a means of reopening sooner. It achieved the former goal in the short-term. Unfortunately, mass screening was unable to suppress the outbreak, let alone eradicate Covid-19. Whereas the mass testing in Wuhan was the final step in a long effort to achieve eradication, the Slovakian testing effort was a once-off intervention during an existing outbreak. Without the long-term resolve, there were limits to what it could achieve.

The critical question is whether screening is a complement to or a substitute for other interventions designed to mitigate outbreaks. When prevalence is low, mass screening can obviate the need for other measures. It is an effective means of finding those needles in the haystack that could grow into outbreaks. When prevalence is high, mass screening can support other measures in bringing reproduction numbers below 1. Thus, there is a difference between introducing mass screening as an insurance measure when R is already below 1 and using it as an active means of breaking transmission chains to bring R from above to below 1. The point is this: Screening must be sustained while the brakes on other activities are applied until an outbreak has been quashed.

This chapter examines how to sustain a screening system through these different phases. The goal is to build the system so that it operates as part of normal life while reducing the risk of the virus sneaking back in. At other times, the system should ensure that outbreaks can be managed. This is precisely what happened at the University of Illinois as was shown in the previous chapter.

There are three sizeable challenges to building a sustainable system. The first is the scale challenge: being able to screen a large portion of a population regularly for a long period of time. The second challenge is convenience: To be sustainable, people need an ultra-convenient way to participate in the screening system. The final challenge is behavioral: We need to pay attention to how people change their behaviors so that those behaviors do not counteract the positive properties of a screening system. In this chapter, I will look at each of these challenges in turn.

The Scale Challenge

The University of Illinois had some things going for it when it established a screening system. First, everyone was in a geographically contained space where, for the most part, people stayed close to the center. Second, even though the population was mobile, they regularly passed screening locations. Third, there was an on-campus infrastructure to store and process tests. Fourth, it was easy to keep records in the university's existing information technology system. Finally, the institution had the ability to implement and enforce a complementary set of sanctions to ensure compliance.[64]

There is a big difference between trying to operate at scale after extensive preparation and trying to operate at scale without preparation. As a case in point, consider Germany's November 2020 attempt to roll out rapid antigen screening to long-term care facilities. The goal was to screen everyone a couple of times per week. The requirements to be able to do so are described here:[65]

> To be able to test residents and others, and receive compensation, care homes are required to produce a "testing concept." This involves defining the groups to be tested; the frequency of testing; the processes involved in administering tests (including the procurement of the tests, training

[64] Similar outcomes were observed across college campuses (Paltiel AD, Zheng A, Walensky RP). Assessment of SARS-CoV-2 Screening Strategies to Permit the Safe Reopening of College Campuses in the United States. *JAMA Netw Open.* 2020;3(7):e2016818. doi:10.1001/jamanetworkopen.2020.16818.

[65] Stefanie Ettelt, "Rapid COVID-19 Testing in Care Homes in Germany: Easier Said Than Done," (LTC Responses to COVID-19, November 24, 2020), https://ltccovid.org/2020/11/24/rapid-covid-19-testing-in-care-homes-in-germany-easier-said-than-done.

requirements, the need for personal protective equipment); and a definition of cases in which an antigen test should be replaced by a PCR test (see example). Care homes have to procure the testing kits themselves. Tests have to meet a set of minimum requirements set out by the Paul Ehrlich Institute and the Federal Office for Pharmaceuticals and Medical Products has published a list of tests available in the market that meet these minimum standards.

The home's testing concept has to be approved by the local health authority in its area, as a condition of reimbursement. Care homes are eligible to receive seven euros per test if they procure the test themselves, for up to twenty tests per resident per month, covering all testing requirements of staff, residents and visitors. Care homes can receive funding for a larger number of tests, if this has been approved by the local health authority as part of the testing concept. Reimbursement is organised through regional associations of office-based doctors (Kassenärztliche Vereinigungen); these organizations routinely organise the reimbursement of services provided by office-based doctors to patients under social health insurance.

You might look at all these requirements and roll your eyes. But, in reality, they are the bare minimum. Basically, it means the care home must know what it is doing, who is going to do it, what protections are needed, and how to procure the screening kits. There are some general guidelines, but to do this within any particular home still requires work. It does not take long for real challenges to kick in.

Care homes need to develop their own testing concept, which is time consuming for both the homes and the local health authorities required to review and approve them. Again, larger organizations such as the Arbeiter-Samariter Bund or Caritas that operate a large number of homes, may have an advantage over smaller entities with less capacity to allocate resources to develop concepts. There have also been reports of local authorities struggling to approve testing concepts at pace, with the city of Bremen bringing in the Medical Service of Social Insurance (MDK) to help.

The testing itself can be done quickly if considering a single test, but doing hundreds or thousands of them per week requires substantial additions [to] staffing and resources. Testing also requires appropriate documentation, which also draws on tight resources. Some care homes have managed to employ additional staff to conduct the testing; however, others reported that they have not been able to employ more staff and that existing staff is already too stretched to engage in additional tasks. There is a general shortage of care personnel in Germany, in both health and long-term care, so it is unlikely that supply will easily match demand. While staff administering tests do not have to be fully medically trained, bespoke training needs to be in place if no medically trained staff is available.

There is not much slack in the system to do this. All of this preparation increases fixed costs, even before the ongoing operational challenges and market constraints of getting screens is included. Even for staff, getting in and out of the workplace probably adds thirty minutes to the day, and someone has to pay for that.

This all illustrates the challenge. To envision rolling out economy-wide, frequent screening is one thing. To actually develop protocols, standard operating procedures, IT infrastructure, testing trials, and best practices for a scaled-up testing system will take time. We might be able to procure screenings within weeks, but moving the process to a sustainable system will likely take months to develop.

Fortunately, there has been some work on this front since August 2020. The Creative Destruction Lab (CDL) is a seed-stage start-up program founded at the University of Toronto. It is now in nine different sites around the world. I serve as its chief economist.

CDL formed the CDL Rapid Screening Consortium,[66] which brought together an initial group of twelve large companies[67] to develop infrastructure and protocols for sustainable screening at workplaces. As of this writing, CDL has evaluated and costed over seventy antigen screens, developed initial protocols, and procured enough screens to run nineteen pilots (with the help of Canadian provincial governments). The pilots are designed to work out operational details and to meet other challenges described below. The hope is that, in a few months, the ingredients will be ready for other workplaces to quickly roll out screening systems. In other words, the work is being done to innovate and explore what needs to be done to meet the scaling challenge.

The Convenience Challenge

Perhaps the most important operational parameter in a screening system is throughput—the number of people who can be screened in the shortest possible time. When a person gets a PCR test, even under the most favorable circumstances, the process will likely take fifteen minutes from start to finish. If there are queues, it will, of course, take much longer. Clearly, if people are going to be screened up to twice per week, inconvenience becomes a real challenge. We need to aim for five minutes or less.

Operational slimming down can help some. However, real constraints exist, and crucial decisions must be made without cutting corners. The goal of testing is to identify infectious people and prevent them from interacting with others. Therefore, we need a system of clearance whereby people are not allowed inside

---

[66] Creative Disruption Lab Rapid Screening Consortium, https://www.cdlrapidscreeningconsortium.com.

[67] Mostly Canadian: Air Canada, Rogers, Loblaws, Shoppers Drug Mart, Magna, Nutrien, Suncor, Genpact, Scotiabank, MDA, CPPIB and MLSE.

certain locations unless they have screened negative. That requires someone to administer the screen and a potentially long wait for results. All of that prolongs inconvenience for those being tested. It can also lead to congestion in the system (i.e., longer queues)— especially problematic during winter if people need to wait outside. These factors make it unlikely that a sustainable system will involve perfect clearance. Some risk will have to be managed.

To give an example of those trade-offs, consider the choice between screening people at the door versus screening them at, for example, an office desk. We often envisage clearance taking place at a door (point of entry). The alternative would be to let people in and then screen them at their desks (or wherever they happen to be). The advantages of this approach are obvious: no waiting at the door and the ability to screen personnel over the course of the day. We would also reduce operational challenges, making the screening system an order of magnitude less costly to run. The disadvantage is also obvious: Infectious people could enter the location and might spread the virus.

The cost-benefit description above, however, is too simplistic. For instance, if we increase the screening frequency among those allowed to enter a location, we could quickly remove infectious individuals. The worst-case scenario is that an infectious person could cause harm for a day. But it would be financially less costly to test everyone at their desks, and we could screen more often. Once you consider all the variables, the best choice becomes less obvious.

Simple calculations help us work out what this means.[68] If the reproduction number is 1.25 (at the high end of levels observed during most of 2020), prevalence in the outside population is one in four thousand. And if the rapid screen has a sensitivity of 85 percent (that is, 15 percent are false negatives), then the outcomes are listed in table 4.1.

---

[68]   Using, say, this calculator: https://steveli.shinyapps.io/
FrequencyAndAccuracyCalculator.

Table 4.1: Expected Number of Infections out of One Thousand after Six Months

	Test every 3 days	Test every 7 days
SCREEN AT DOOR	14	51
SCREEN AT DESK	28	81

You can see that, for a given frequency, screening at the door results in fewer internally spread infections than screening at the desk. But if screening at the desk can be done more frequently than screening at the door, then you end up with fewer infections. Therefore, if screening at the desk costs 50 percent less than screening at the door, then, for the same cost, we can reduce the number of infections by screening at the desk.[69]

In summary, we have more options than just focusing on minimizing the number of infections. If we think about the whole board of options, we can see that a system might involve more convenience and less risk.

The Behavioral Challenge

If someone is screened and found to be positive, the system works if that person is isolated and then proceeds for follow-up with the relevant health system. As we saw earlier, initially, at the University of Illinois, this did not happen; the system had to be modified to ensure compliance. This is an illustration of the behavioral challenge that arises in any sustainable screening system.

---

[69] This is all without doing other things. For instance, contact tracing if someone gets through who is positive, or a hybrid system in which those who are deemed to be more at risk or who work in closed quarters, are screened at the door while others are screened at the desk. There are many options available and, for each, we can model the costs and benefits.

This particular issue has proved important when thinking about where screens are performed. Harvard's Michael Mina, who has recently been pushing for cheap, frequent testing, has likened testing options to a Nespresso coffee machine (buy a testing machine and test people in the workplace) or instant coffee (make coffee cheaply at home). He advocates the latter, arguing for people to take the test and, if positive, to stay at home. This would certainly be convenient and cost-efficient. There would be no queues and no bottlenecks with people who have to administer screens. The problem, however, is that such convenience and cost savings create compliance risks.

Consider this. Suppose you have an important flight. You take the test at home and it is positive. What then? Do you go to take the flight anyhow? If you are asked to self-report your test results, that is an option. But if the flight is important or not refundable or something, your incentives get all screwed up.

The solution to this is obvious: Airlines could require people take a test at the airport. That makes sense, but health screens and the like, especially if they are consequential as we intend them to be in this scenario, can encroach on privacy laws.

Nonetheless, at-home or self-administered screens face trust problems. Can we rely on people to properly self-administer a screen and then do the right thing? We already face this challenge with symptom checking and yet we have chosen to rely on self-administration. Ironically, we do this by asking people to fill out a form (on paper or an app) confirming they have checked their symptoms. Did they actually do it? Nobody knows for sure, even though they did the paperwork. In reality, the paperwork is merely a nudge to spend a few seconds thinking about Covid-19 symptoms before heading out, and if they seem to have symptoms, to think about whether it is worth going out or if anyone will notice.

What is the difference if someone were to self-administer a Covid-19 screen? One issue is that the person might perform the screen incorrectly. In that case, the main risk is not getting a false positive but a false negative. The self-administered test might not pick up (literally) enough of the right type of sample to detect the virus. That means the person might confidently, but errantly, interact with others. So, there is every reason to believe that self-administered screens would empower unwitting spreaders.[70]

Like a symptom check, a positive screening result creates tension for the person involved. Unlike a symptom check, a positive screening result leaves the person with no excuses (i.e., it could be the cold or the flu). That person should reasonably conclude that he or she has Covid-19, should isolate and/or receive a confirmatory PCR test, and should visit a medical professional to work out next steps. Consider how an economist might weigh up that individual quandary.

- Need for treatment: Covid-19 is a scary disease. Those who screen frequently and receive a positive result in the early stages of the disease should take action to get ahead of it. Those who get a positive screen have an incentive to go through the official process.

- Protecting others: Knowledge of a positive screening result indicates potential infectiousness. Out of concern for others and fear of the consequences associated with not caring about them should lead people to self-isolate, at the very least.[71]

- Protecting yourself: Someone with Covid-19 can't get more Covid-19 (at least not soon). So, for infected people, there is no longer a *self-protection* reason to restrict activity. In this case, there could be an incentive to carry on normally.

Putting it this way, slowing the spread of disease involves social

---

[70] I should add here that there is a George Costanza issue in that you may claim you are positive even if you screen negative to get out of going to work or school. But the risk is you can only claim that once so what happens if you actually get Covid-19?

[71] This is the route emphasized in a recent paper. Source: Thomas F. Hellmann and Veikko Thiele, "A Theory of Voluntary Testing and Self-Isolation in an Ongoing Pandemic," (National Bureau of Economic Research, no. w27941, M2020).

trust issues. We hope that people will believe in and act on the first two options, not the last one. The first option involves a private, self-care motive. The second involves an altruistic motive (concern for others). The third involves a divergence between private motives and social consequences; in other words, the failure to internalize an externality. Not surprisingly, it is the one many economists worry about.

Here's what is interesting: We know something about the people who might prefer the third reason more than the first two in their decisions. They are the people who are most fearful of going out to interact with others without a screening. Why are they fearful? Because they also care about getting treatment and/ or protecting others. Indeed, a recent paper found that with respect to Covid-19, those who were at most risk of poor health outcomes from Covid-19 were more likely to practice social distancing.[72] These are presumably people who would also be motivated to seek treatment if they knew they were positive.

In other words, people sort themselves into clusters of different types. It is rare to find people who are only motivated by the third reason, but it is common to find people who are motivated by the first two reasons, and vice versa. In broad terms, people either care about all three, or they care about none of them. Either way, it is far from obvious that someone who receives a positive screening result will decide that he or she is safe to attend a large party. Why? Precisely because that person will have already chosen not to party or is already partying. A positive screen is not going to change a person's behavior drastically in terms of risk to others. Again, very few people are motivated by option three. Thus, it is a reasonable to conclude that people who worry about trust are worrying about the type of person who rarely exists.

---

[72] M. Eichenbaum, M.G. de Matos, F. Lima, S. Rebelo, and M. Trabandt, "How Do People Respond to Small Probability Events with Large, Negative Consequences?" (CEPR Discussion Papers, no. 15573, 2020).

All that said, we don't have to implement widespread screening in a vacuum. We could rely primarily on self-administered screens with occasional check-ins to assess compliance. What this suggests is that to automatically rule out self-administration does not seem warranted, especially given the speed and potential logistical advantages of operating that way.

One final observation on the behavioral challenge: If the system works at scale, that itself will change behavior. After all, if we know that everyone who is out and about has been screened recently and is unlikely to be infectious with Covid-19, then we are less likely to worry about protecting ourselves from them. That means less social distancing and other measures. Of course, if *everyone* thinks that way, including those who have just received positive screening results, then the value of the screening system itself will be mitigated. This is called the rebound effect, which I discussed in *The Pandemic Information Gap*. The idea of rebounds is the economist's go-to theory for explaining why "there may be bad unintended consequences." It often appears in the first chapter of Econ101 textbooks. It's not why economics was called the "dismal science," but it is why people often think of economists as dismal.

Broadly speaking, the theory says, "on the one hand" screening and isolation reduce the epidemiological spread of the virus for a given level of social activity. But then we say, "on the other hand" people know with whom they have interacted and who among them has screened negative, so they don't fear those interactions. One effect pushes infections down while the other counteracts that effect.[73] The problem is that if screening is not 100 percent perfect or ubiquitous, which it won't be, we can't be sure that the end result won't be more infections.

In summary, when we roll out widespread screening, we can't

---

[73] Joshua S. Gans, "The Economic Consequences of R = 1: Towards a Workable Behavioral Epidemiological Model of Pandemics," (NBER Working Paper Series, w27632, 2020).

assume people will act in a compliant way for the sake of others. Instead, we must plan for the opposite, lest we undermine all of our good intentions.[74]

Complacency

A question that often arises in relation to screening systems is: What about the White House? There were significant Covid-19 outbreaks and infections there, including an infection of the person at the top. Does this prove that screening systems don't work?

Those questions raise an excellent point. The one place, literally in the world, that has the resources and the motivation to manage an on-going information problem is the White House. To keep the virus out of there requires constant, daily testing of all personnel along with ensuring that people act safely, although not necessarily perfectly, outside the White House. The White House just needs to ensure that anyone in direct contact with the president goes through a testing regime. Do all of that and everyone should be able to operate normally inside the bubble.

However, Covid-19 spread through the White House. Some staff members then started to blame the tests. This is from *The New York Times*:[75]

> For months, the White House's strategy for keeping President Trump and his inner circle safe has been to screen all White House visitors with a rapid test.

---

[74] In November 2020, Liverpool ran a pilot to offer rapid antigen screens for its entire population of five hundred thousand. About a third took them up on it and the result, as occurred in Slovakia, was a reduction in infections immediately following the trial. That study also had some findings regarding behavior. It found that people were unlikely to change their risk-taking behavior following a negative screen but that, following a positive screen, they did not obtain a confirmatory PCR test until they received explicit reminders to do so. University of Liverpool, "Liverpool Covid-SMART Pilot Evaluation," (December 1, 2020), https://www.liverpool.ac.uk/coronavirus/research-and-analysis/covid-smart-pilot.

[75] Apoorva Mandavilli, "The White House Relied on a Rapid Test, but Used It in a Way It Was not Intended," *The New York Times*, October 2, 2020.

But one product they use, Abbott's ID Now, was never intended for that purpose and is known to deliver incorrect results. In issuing an emergency use authorization, the Food and Drug Administration said the test was only to be used by a health care provider 'within the first seven days of symptoms.'

The ID Now has several qualities in its favor: It's portable, doesn't need skilled technicians to operate and delivers results in fifteen minutes. Used to evaluate someone with symptoms, the test can quickly and easily diagnose Covid-19, the disease caused by the coronavirus.

But in people who are infected but not yet showing symptoms, the test is much less accurate, missing as many as one in three cases.

Of course, as we learned in chapter 2, rapid antigen tests are quite accurate for determining whether someone is infectious, which is what you want for a screening system. Moreover, the ID Now test used was a PCR test, but one that gave results in only fifteen minutes. That test, however, had very high sensitivity when people had more than a minimal viral load.

In the White House, it is possible that samples were collected in different ways than normally occur for an ordinary PCR test. However, studies have shown that when viral loads are high, using a shorter nasal swab to obtain samples or some dilution of those samples to speed up testing would not appreciably reduce sensitivity.[76] It is not publicly known, precisely, how the White House collected samples.[77] But these studies indicate that the sample collecting method should not have mattered so long as

---

[76] Atreyee Basu, Tatyana Zinger, Kenneth Inglima, Kar-mun Woo, Onomie Atie, Lauren Yurasits, Benjamin See, and Maria E. Aguero-Rosenfeld, "Performance of the Rapid Nucleic Acid Amplification by Abbott ID NOW Covid-19 in Nasopharyngeal Swabs Transported in Viral Media and Dry Nasal Swabs, in a New York City Academic Institution," *BioRxiv* (2020), https://www.biorxiv.org/content/10.1101/2020.05.11.089896v1.full.

[77] One suspects that if it were the uncomfortable long nasal swabs that may have been at the heart of the matter.

people were being tested routinely and frequently. Moreover, if that had been done, it should have been possible to hold meetings outdoors without masks for a couple of hours.

The challenge of a screening protocol in a high-risk environment is that it is fragile. If there is one person who comes into contact with any others who are not being tested frequently, the entire system can break down. If there are many untested people, the virus can get into the bubble and spread quickly. For this to have happened at the White House, the most likely cause was that people were not adhering to protocols. Testing was likely not happening daily. People were too busy.

But we knew people in the White House would be busy. We knew those people would think there was an exception. To prevent those exceptions in that environment, *everyone* needed to cede authority. Put simply, because the White House is a high-stress environment, the right frame of mind should have been to treat everyone inside as a four-year-old—*everyone.* To force compliance with the Covid-19 prevention rules, everyone should have been presumed to be a child. Then a nagging parent with authority should have been installed at all points of entry.

My point is this: In terms of disease prevention, it is dangerous to think of the White House as exceptional. It is not. The dangers that White House staff put themselves into are the dangers that everyone else without resources and lines of authority can face. A place of business that can remain open because of a screening protocol should have someone who can prevent every entry, including by the CEO, unless those who seek to enter have been tested. This especially holds for airline travel. Perhaps ironically, the places where such complacency is less likely to cause problems is schools. This is because everyone, including the children, knows who needs extra monitoring.

Many organizations might need to take a long, hard look at their practices and see if they have a robust protocol that accounts for complacency. From my perspective, that means an *ultimate*

Covid-19-prevention authority. As every parent knows, that is easier said than done.

The White House needed to have strict protocols. The dangers of not having them were too great. From just a national security perspective, the lack of strict protocols would have made it remarkably easy for someone to intentionally spread Covid-19 inside. Unfortunately, it is apparent that White House personnel did not adhere to the protocols.

For the rest of us, the lesson is the ultimate cautionary tale. This crisis is ongoing. We do not have the opportunity to let our guard down. We have to become our own nagging parents and work out ways to keep that up. There is room for substantial innovation, and it will certainly be my priority to think about how to implement good screening protocols.

5

Surveillance Data

Testing and screening as potential solutions to the pandemic information gap all involve identifying individuals who are more likely to be infectious and then isolating them. But information can also be gathered at broader levels to inform us about more targeted interventions. In one of her great statements during this crisis, New Zealand Prime Minister Jacinda Ardern said:

> We currently have 102 cases. But so did Italy once. Now the virus has overwhelmed their health system and hundreds of people are dying every day. The situation here is moving at pace, and so must we.[78]

Her point was that an early warning to act was better than waiting until local conditions reached a worse stage. Pandemic management requires doing everything possible to obtain information quickly so that a response can be enacted quickly.

This chapter considers surveillance. What are the ways governments and others can obtain the information they need so as to take actions that preempt viral spread? The answer can help

---

[78] Newshub, "Coronavirus: Prime Minister Jacinda Ardern's Full Covid-19 Speech," (March 23, 2020), https://www.newshub.co.nz/home/politics/2020/03/coronavirus-prime-minister-jacinda-ardern-s-full-covid-19-speech.html.

us avoid reacting to outbreaks when they are already prevalent, and when those actions are more costly and less effective. The less information we have about the location of viral outbreaks, the more widespread our subsequent interventions—in particular, lockdowns—will have to be. By obtaining surveillance data quickly, interventions can be deployed that have a lower economic and social cost.

Eyes on the Internet

Most surveillance regarding potential outbreaks comes from governments reporting about what is going on in their countries. However, there are conflicts of interest. Public reports of infectious disease outbreaks can impact adversely on local economies. In some cases, such reports might undermine the political interests of those governments. This is not to say that such information is not useful. It is. But given the potential global ramifications of outbreaks, we also need information from disinterested parties.

This is when the Internet has proved useful. One source of information is Google. Google had previously tried to get ahead of local flu outbreaks with Google Flu Trends, which used individual searches for "flu medication" and the like to identify potential outbreaks. Unfortunately, their algorithm was not robust from year to year thereby undermining the ability to provide an automated forecast of potential issues. Nonetheless, a similar ability to detect Covid-19 regional outbreaks was possible. Figure 5.1 shows, as an example, US searches in 2020 for things like "loss of smell," which arises under the general topic of anosmia. Loss of smell is a now known to be a frequent symptom of Covid-19. The broad contours of the trend matched the patterns of Covid-19's spread in the US. Thus, when confirmed cases are potentially missed, such searches can fill the information gap.[79]

Researchers have shown that by analyzing Internet data they can open a "window" on the pandemic to see leading indicators of cases.[80] This opportunity has been known for many years and was, in fact, the underlying thesis of a very worthwhile Canadian initiative called the Global Public Health Intelligence Network (GPHIN).

GPHIN was created as an experiment in the 1990s to use the Internet to gather information that might signal public health

Figure 5.1: Google Trends Search for Anosmia in the US (November 2020)

[79]   Others showed that Amazon reviews for scented candles—with reviewers complaining of no scent—also tracked Covid-19 patterns. Source: Joshua S. Gans, "Looking for Covid-19 in Other Places," (December 7, 2020), https://joshuagans.substack.com/p/looking-for-covid-19-in-other-places.

[80]   Cornelia Ilin, Sébastien Annan-Phan, Xiao Hui Tai, Shikhar Mehra, Solomon Hsiang, and Joshua Evan Blumenstock, "Public Mobility Data Enables Covid-19 Forecasting and Management at Local and Global Scales," (NBER Working Paper Series w28120, 2020).

problems, including potential pandemics. The inspiration was news reporting of the 1994 epidemic of pneumonic plague in Surat, India.[81] But it became a cornerstone of Canada's pandemic preparation infrastructure after the SARS outbreak in 2003.

> With a team of roughly a dozen highly specialized analysts working in multiple languages, GPHIN was globally renowned for its ability to collect and disseminate credible information. It scoured more than seven thousand data points a day, including medical data, news reports, scraps of information on social media, and details on Internet blogs to gather intelligence on outbreaks.

> GPHIN had been credited with detecting some of the most important signals from the 2009 H1N1 outbreak in Mexico, outbreaks of Zika in West Africa, and a potentially catastrophic 2005 bird flu outbreak that the Iranian government tried to hide. As recently as two years ago, the WHO credited the Canadian unit for supplying 20 percent of its "epidemiological intelligence."[82]

Google leaders were impressed and offered to purchase GPHIN from the Canadian government in 2008.[83] Another initiative, ProMED, was an email list used by people to provide reports and signals to one another. GPHIN's search was broader in scope and did not rely on subscriber contributions. To ensure that information was credible, a partnership with the World Health Organization (WHO) was set up in 2001.

---

[81] E. Mykhalovskiy and L. Weir, "The Global Public Health Intelligence Network and Early Warning Outbreak Detection: A Canadian Contribution to Global Public Health," *Canadian Journal of Public Health*, 97, no. 1, (January-February 2006): 42-44, https://doi.org/10.1007/BF03405213.

[82] Grant Roberson, "Health Minister Orders Review of Pandemic Warning System, Concerns Raised by Scientists," *The Globe and Mail*, September 7, 2020, https://www.theglobeandmail.com/canada/article-health-minister-orders-review-of-pandemic-warning-system-concerns.

[83] Grant Robertson, "'Without Early Warning You Can't Have Early Response: How Canada's World-Class Pandemic Alert System failed," *The Globe and Mail,* July 25, 2020, https://www.theglobeandmail.com/canada/article-without-early-warning-you-cant-have-early-response-how-canadas.

SARS was the real validating event of this approach. GPHIN issued the first alert of an unusual respiratory illness in Guangdong Province, China, in November 2002. This was enough to put the WHO on alert with further information coming from GPHIN in February 2003, prompting of an official Chinese government response. In 2005, it was Iran's turn after GPHIN discovered notices telling people to call officials if they discovered a dead bird. Iran acknowledged the bird flu outbreak six months later.

> In 2009, analysts alerted the WHO to an H1N1 swine flu pandemic in Mexico, after studying reports of unusual illnesses near Veracruz, where stores were suddenly selling out of bleach. It was only after the WHO contacted the Mexican Ministry of Health that the problem was publicly acknowledged.

> The alerts worked like a smoke detector ensuring governments were at least aware of potentially urgent situations. Not every signal became a crisis, but the system never seemed to miss a big one. It was soon endorsed by the WHO as a crucial service—the 'cornerstone' of Canada's pandemic response capability, and 'the foundation' of global early warning, where signals are 'rapidly acted upon' and 'trigger a cascade of actions' by governments, the organization said.[84]

GPHIN has played a similar role since, detecting early indicators of the 2009 H1N1 outbreak and the 2012 MERS epidemic.[85] On average, until 2019, GPHIN issued a dozen alerts per month.

The story from there should have been how GPHIN discovered earlier signs of a novel coronavirus. With a budget of just CAD2.8 million per year, the program was cheap. But that didn't stop it from being subject to budget cuts and changes in how the Public

---

[84] Ibid.

[85] M. Dion, P. Abdel Malik, A. Mawudeku, "Big Data and the Global Public Health Intelligence Network (GPHIN)," *Canadian Communicable Disease Report* 41, no. 9, (September 3, 2015): 209-214, https://doi.org/10.14745/ccdr.v41i09a02.

Health Agency of Canada was managed.[86] The service was no longer scientist-run and approvals started to delay warnings. Many who ran the system left the agency. After May 24, 2019, no further alerts were issued. The system went dark. According to an investigation by *The Globe and Mail,* this all happened without notifying the international community of the change.[87] Following the media alert, in August 2020, GHPIN began issuing alerts again.[88]

This is a story about the potential value of this type of surveillance, and also a cautionary tale about how important it is that surveillance be allowed to continue and be managed in an independent manner. With mobile data and social media, the efficacy of using the Internet to provide early signals of pandemic related problems is higher than ever.[89]

Eyes on the Sewers

GPHIN wasn't an automated process. It relied on algorithms to serve up items of interest. A team of experts sifted through that information before alerts were issued. Now there are opportunities to use automation to provide surveillance data. One method is to monitor sewage for the presence of the coronavirus. This allows public health officials to monitor the locations of possible outbreaks and, therefore, where containment efforts should be focused.

---

[86] Grant Robertson, "'We Are Not Prepared': The Flaws Inside Public Health That Hurt Canada's Readiness for Covid-19," *The Globe and Mail,* December 26, 2020, https://www.theglobeandmail.com/canada/article-we-are-not-prepared-the-flaws-inside-public-health-that-hurt-canadas.

[87] Robertson, op.cit., July 25, 2020.

[88] Grant Robertson, "Canada's International Pandemic Alert Back in Operation, More Than 400 Days After Falling Silent," *The Globe and Mail,* August 13, 2020, https://www.theglobeandmail.com/canada/article-canadas-international-pandemic-alert-back-in-action-more-than-40.

[89] W. Wang W, Y. Wang, X. Zhang, X. Jia, Y. Li, S. Dang, "Using WeChat, a Chinese Social Media App, for Early Detection of the Covid-19 Outbreak in December 2019: Retrospective Study," *JMIR Mhealth Uhealth* 8, no. 10, (October 5, 2020), https://doi.org/10.2196/19589.

In May 2020, Yale researchers published a paper that showed the potential for sewage sludge to be used as a leading indicator of Covid-19 outbreaks.[90] You'd think that it would be hard to find coronavirus RNA unless you collected a ton of sewage, but no. They found it all over the place. Moreover, when adjusting for time lags, what they found was highly correlated with health data on Covid-19 cases and hospital admissions in New Haven, Connecticut and surrounding areas. The data allowed them to see a problem three days before hospital admissions and seven days before testing data, if there was an outbreak.[91]

One can imagine a situation in which PCR testing might be automated at the location where samples can be collected. That could provide real-time monitoring of potential outbreaks.[92] A wastewater treatment plant usually covers a wide area. It provides real early warning of issues, but a more granular system might be preferable. Researchers at the University of Toronto and elsewhere have discovered a way to do just that.[93]

Their innovation is twofold. First, they collect data at sewer-system maintenance holes. That is easier said than done as there are lots of maintenance holes and they are all interconnected. So, the second innovation involves algorithms to sort through the potential mess.

The data source is wastewater that is sampled and real-time tested from selected maintenance holes. The algorithms

---

[90] Jordan Peccia, Alessandro Zulli, Doug E. Brackney, et al., "SARS-CoV-2 RNA Concentrations in Primary Municipal Sewage Sludge As a Leading Indicator of Covid-19 Outbreak Dynamics," *medRxiv*, (June 12, 2020), https://doi.org/10.1101/2020.05.19.201059 99.

[91] One interesting part of the research is that it did not require a large sample. The "[s]ludge collected from ESWPAF is primary sludge, sampled at the outlet of a gravity thickener, ranging in solids content from 2.6% to 5%" and they used ‹2.5 mL of well mixed sludge' to extract RNA from. On this, they conducted a standard PCR test on the sludge. The test turned out to be quite sensitive.

[92] A startup called Nanopath, founded by researchers from Dartmouth, has developed the potential for rapid automation of PCR tests for Covid-19 and other viruses.

[93] R.C. Larson, O. Berma, M. Nourinejad, "Sampling Manholes to Home In on SARS-CoV-2 Infections," *PLoS ONE* 15, no. 10, (October 5, 2020), https://doi.org/10.1371/journal.pone.0240007.

dynamically and adaptively develop a sequence of maintenance holes to sample and test. The algorithms are often finished after five to ten maintenance hole samples, meaning that—in the field—the procedure can be carried out within one day. The goal is to provide timely information that will support faster, more productive human testing for viral infection and thus reduce community disease spread.

Put simply, by collecting data closer to the source, information can be generated more rapidly than by waiting for it to flow downstream to treatment plants. They write:

> Any test of the upstream manhole, if it exists, would reveal no Covid-19 from the residence of the infected person(s). But the closest downstream manhole would provide that evidence. We seek to find that closest downstream manhole. If successful, we can then reduce our search for the infected person(s) to residences of only a few houses (i.e., all those houses first inputting to the same downstream manhole). By such targeted human testing, we may be able to stop any spread from Patient(s) Zero to the rest of the community.

This is quite a challenging process:

> Leveraging the tree graph structure of the sewage system, we develop two algorithms, the first designed for a community that is certified at a given time to have zero infections and the second for a community known to have many infections. For the first, we assume that wastewater at the WTP has just revealed traces of SARS-CoV-2, indicating existence of a "Patient Zero" in the community. This first algorithm identifies the city block in which the infected person resides. For the second, we home in on a most infected neighborhood of the community, where a neighborhood is usually several city blocks.

It is certainly fascinating and shows the potential of using sophisticated statistical techniques to provide a deeper understanding of outbreaks.

Not surprisingly, we need a solid sampling process for maintenance holes, and good mapping data on the nature of the system. The researchers show how this can be done for a small New England town. In the end, using a Bayesian framework, the researchers show how to convert sewage flows into "probability flows" to assess the right place to collect samples. Suffice it to say that those in the business of collecting stool want to optimize anything they can. With their algorithm, they can find a hotspot neighborhood with as few as four samples. Finding Patient Zero in a new outbreak is a little harder, but ten samples will do the job.

That said, this approach does presume relatively stable depositing behavior by people in the town. The authors recognize this but have yet to work out how to deal with it.

> We did not devote attention to evaluating the relative Bayesian probabilities. Their careful estimation for this procedure could be an entirely separate paper, and in practice, could result in much-improved performance. For instance, a neighborhood in which the majority of people have jobs that require leaving the house and working in an environment with substantial human interaction is likely to generate more Covid-19 cases than one in which most residents can work from home via the Internet. These differences can be expressed by markedly different values of the Bayesian probabilities assigned to neighborhoods.

There is work to be done. But there is certainly potential for monitoring sewage systems to provide a window on potential outbreaks.[94]

---

[94] Some of this has begun to take place with the CDC's creation of a National Wastewater Surveillance System. Source: Kim Tingley, "Watching What We Flush Could Help Keep a Pandemic Under Control," *The New York Times,* November 24, 2020.

Eyes on the Virus

Covid-19 monitoring usually takes the form of tracking confirmed cases—cases where there is a positive PCR test. The difficulty with this measure is that it might miss cases when asymptomatic spreaders do not suspect they have Covid-19. For this reason, the positivity rate—the proportion of all tests administered that are positive—is viewed as an indicator of the reliability of confirmed case statistics. That is, if positivity is high, it is likely that many cases are being missed. A low positivity rate (less than one or two out of every hundred tested) indicates that the case counts are reliable. As an outbreak waxes and wanes, these rates change, but case counts can be correspondingly adjusted. Nonetheless, these indicators are imperfect.

Knowing more about those cases can help considerably. One way would be to have regular genetic identification of coronavirus variants. Like any virus, the novel coronavirus mutates, and some mutations spread while others do not. From the perspective of tracking, this can be useful information. The company Biohub has successfully used genetic information to enable better decision-making.

> Last week, in Northern California, a pair of workers at a fish-packing plant came down with symptoms of Covid-19. The Biohub processed their tests and found both workers had the virus. In an age not all that distant from ours, the fish-packing plant, which believed it had taken the measures to keep its workers safe, would have been forced to close, as it would have had to assume that one of the workers had infected the other on the job. But then Joe DeRisi's Badass Virus Hunters sequenced the two viruses and showed they were genetically far apart: The two workers had contracted the virus independently and outside of work. The fish-packing plant was able to stay open—and its workers were

able to stay on their jobs.[95]

In other words, by using genetic information, we could find evidence of outbreaks, take preventative action, and allow economic activity to continue. In other situations, more virulent strains of the virus can be tracked using genetic information. This is what was happening in January 2021, as countries tracked a variant of SARS-CoV-2 that was potentially 50 percent more infectious than older strains.

Understanding more about the virus actually carried by individuals can assist in surveillance as well. As mentioned in chapter 2, the Ct score in a PCR test can give us an indication of the viral load in an infected person. That viral load follows a pattern such as that depicted in figure 2.3. It peaks at about four or five days after infection and drops thereafter for a couple of weeks. Importantly, the ramp up and ramp down are not symmetric.

A recent paper shows that we could use just one day of PCR test data from infected people in a population to precisely map the dynamics of the virus.[96] At present, just looking at the total numbers of cases does not give us a real indication as to the future path of the virus. Of course, by taking the same people and measuring their viral loads, we would see some indication. The paper provides us with a shortcut to that information. If we had the Ct score for all of those tests, and if the virus is steady—not expanding or contracting—it is likely that the aggregate pattern of scores would look like a blown-up version of figure 2.4. By contrast, if the virus is spreading, the aggregate pattern would be skewed to the left as relatively more people would be in the early stages of infection. If the pattern is skewed right, the opposite would be true.

After running simulations, results could be compared with

95 Michael Lewis, "The New Weapon in the Covid-19 War," *Bloomberg Opinion*, June 22, 2020.

96 James A. Hay, Lee Kennedy-Shaffer, Sanjat Kanjilal, Marc Lipsitch, Michael J. Mina, "Estimating Epidemiologic Dynamics from Single Cross-Sectional Viral Load Distributions," *medRxiv*, (October 3, 2020), https://doi.org/10.1101/2020.10.08.20204222.

hospital data that includes the Ct score. When the two match, we could get data that properly identifies the most significant population-level number, the reproduction number, for the coronavirus. This could occur without widespread testing, and right at the moment, which is better than waiting for a time-series pattern to emerge. Of course, to do this would require collecting and then reporting Ct scores with every positive test result. As mentioned in chapter 2, there is currently resistance to doing that.

Eyes on the Networks

Better information allows us to deploy targeted and nuanced policies to combat pandemics. Absent that information, with only broad aggregate statistics, widespread lockdowns and closures of places like schools need to be employed. For instance, in the second half of 2020, officials in Melbourne imposed a widespread lockdown of the city and its suburbs, even when data showed that outbreaks were concentrated in only a few localities. This occurred because the government lacked information regarding how people moved across the city. If the officials had had that information, they might have been able to use a more targeted approach.

Recent research has shown that a virus might spread in distinct ways, depending on the locality. Recall that the goal of lockdowns is not to lock down per se, but to restrict activities so as to contain viral spread in the general population while also imposing minimal economic cost. If every location were similar, we could set national guidelines and that would be that. But recent research shows the opposite.

Figure 5.2: Illustrative Example of Contact Network and Social Distance Policies

(a) *Normal configuration, two firms, two schools*

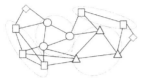

(b) *Schools shut down and red firm shuts down*

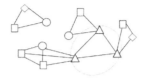

(c) *All firms and schools shut down*

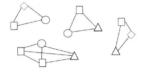

(d) *Work from home when possible, no schools*

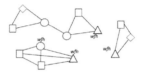

Note: The figure displays a stylized example of a network of heterogeneous individuals grouped in households, schools, and firms, under different policies, where 1a is the configuration during normal times. Green squares nodes correspond to children, red circles correspond to workers of a manufacturing firm, black triangles to workers of a tech firm, and blue diamonds indicate individuals who are not working. In panel 1b red firm and schools are closed, in panel 1c all firms and schools are closed, and in panel 1d schools are closed and those who can work from home, while others are allowed to go to work.

The network structure of cities matters.[97] Different policies have different impacts on network structures. Figure 5.2 is illustrative. It shows hypothetical links between children (squares), manufacturing workers (circles), and service workers (triangles). If we keep firms and schools open, we sustain many links between them and everyone remains connected. Shut schools and the manufacturing plant down, and we sever lots of those links, but not all of them. A full lockdown divides the economy into the smallest number of components; that is, groups of people who are connected with each other but not others outside their groups. And then there is work from home (for service firms), closed manufacturing, and

---

[97]   Mohammad Akbarpour, Cody Cook, Aude Marzuoli, Simon Mongey, Abhishek Nagaraj, Matteo Saccarola, Pietro Tebaldi, Shoshana Vasserman, and Hanbin Yang, "Socioeconomic Network Heterogeneity and Pandemic Policy Response," (University of Chicago, Becker Friedman Institute for Economics Working Paper 2020-75, 2020), https://abhishekn.com/files/network-heterogeneity-pandemic-policy.pdf.

closed schools. We end up with more connections than a complete lockdown, but we still have fewer components. Moreover, those who are connected are connected by a single link. Some argue that option d is the best compromise between economic value and health safety, and that there is little to be gained in the latter by going to option c.

That's the theory. But what the research shows is that different US cities really differ in their networks. One model takes into account age (including the various health impacts of Covid-19 on age), work patterns, commuting patterns, population density, and the ability to work from home. Then it compares employment with the expected death outcomes of various policies that are anchored to a cautious reopening. (Most cities are reopening in ways that limit interactions but that allow people to go about their business.) There are five types of policies: cautious reopening (CR); essential only (EO); work from home if possible (WFH); isolate those over age sixty (60+); and alternating schedules (AS). In the case of AS, students and workers are split into two groups that don't interact and alternate days coming in. The trade-offs between these policies differ between cities. A WFH policy generally outperforms both 60+ and CR on both key dimensions. In Chicago and New York, moving from WFH to AS to EO reduces deaths but at the expense of higher unemployment. But in Sacramento, there is no health safety benefit from other policies and so WFH is unambiguously the best policy.

What should we make of this? First, there are big returns for gathering the data necessary to understand city network structure. For instance, if Sacramento officials had used New York data, and if they had believed they could reduce deaths by 10 percent by going to EO from WFH, they would be disappointed to learn from the model that there would have been no reduction in deaths and a doubling of employment losses. Second, understanding these issues does not require ongoing surveillance. The network structure and demographics of cities are pretty stable over time. Thus, we need only investigate once in a while to get enough information. Then we could assess the trade-offs of different policies over time as the prevalence of the disease changes.[98]

My point is that information could be gathered during normal, non-pandemic times and used to inform us about the best policies for each area. Information gathered during normal times could be paired with data collected during a pandemic to assist in understanding how pandemics spread.

As an example, consider the Covid-19 tragedies that befell many long-term care and nursing homes. Economists Keith Chen and Judy Chevalier, and medical researcher Elisa Long, explored the patterns of movements in and out of nursing homes across several US states.[99] They collected data from smartphones to determine where people who visited nursing homes also went. The answer: Based on a sample of thirty million phones, 7 percent of those who visited one nursing home also visited another. And that 7 percent was observed visiting multiple nursing homes after the restrictions in March had prohibited such behaviors.

Why is this significant? As we know, Covid-19 spreads through contacts—most likely between people who are breathing the same air for a certain period of time indoors. Because nursing home interactions occur indoors, prevalence might be high. The related fatality rate is because residents of nursing homes are particularly vulnerable to complications from Covid-19.

The researchers for the paper found that these connections and their numbers strongly predict Covid-19 outbreaks in nursing homes. The paper indicates that employees traveled between nursing homes. Nurses have a median salary of $28,000 from one job, so it isn't surprising that many take on shifts elsewhere to make ends meet. The researchers found that increased connectedness increased

---

[98]   The data is available and being updated here: https://reopenmappingproject.com.

[99]   M. Keith Chen, Judith A. Chevalier, and Elisa F. Long, "Nursing Home Staff Networks and Covid-19," *Proceedings of the National Academy of Sciences* 118, no. 1, (2020).

Covid-19 cases. Specifically, ten more workers with at least one connection led to a 26 percent rise in cases, and ten more contacts within a connection led to another 12.1 percent rise. Weight these and the result is a 30.7 percent increase in cases. If we compare the state with the fewest connections to the state with the most connections, we find that the latter has 190 percent more cases.[100] The action item is clear: Nursing homes have to create staff bubbles to stop inter-home connections. Do this and we could potentially reduce infections by 44 percent.

Having network information can also assist in other stages of a pandemic. For instance, surveillance should not end when vaccines are available and being distributed. Many consider the value of vaccines in terms of their protection for people, but vaccines can also—in certain cases (such as with the HPV vaccine)[101]—prevent viral shedding and reduce the spread of a disease. In this situation, it makes sense to use the network to target those people in society who are most responsible for spreading so as to mitigate outbreaks more rapidly. This would actually do more to protect the most vulnerable from Covid-19's harm to health.[102]

To achieve this, however, relies upon (a) knowing who the spreaders are and (b) whether the vaccine does, in fact, prevent spreading. We can obtain knowledge about the spreaders from network data. As to whether the vaccine prevents spreading, we can learn more by testing those who have been vaccinated. Sadly, both types of information have been missing during the Covid-19 pandemic. The Covid-19 vaccines have been distributed according

---

[100] This finding comports with research on Europe and US states that showed that countries/states, where long-term care beds per capita (controlling for demography) were lower, had much lower fatality rates; Neil Gandal et al., "Long-Term Care Facilities As a Risk Factor for Death Due to COVID-19: Evidence from European Countries and U.S. States," (SSRN, July 2, 2020), https://ssrn.com/abstract=3616760.

[101] Adam Finn and Richard Malley, "A Vaccine That Stops Covid-19 Won't Be Enough," *The New York Times*, August 24, 2020; https://www.nytimes.com/2020/08/24/opinion/coronavirus-vaccine-prevention.html?searchResultPosition=3.

[102] Laura Matrajt, Julie Eaton, Tiffany Leung, and Elizabeth R. Brown, "Vaccine Optimization for Covid-19, Who to Vaccinate First?" *medRxiv* (2020).

to ad hoc rules similar to those used to distribute the flu vaccine rather than by procedures tailored for this pandemic.[103]

It Starts with the Data

To achieve proper surveillance in a pandemic, it is critical to maintain quality data. This requires security, quality assurance, and continual vigilance. A case in point is what happened in the UK when data went missing in October 2020.

Because of my interest in artificial intelligence, people often ask me what Big Data is. In order to be more precise than saying "a ton of data," I now say, "too much data to be handled by an Excel spreadsheet." That is because an Excel spreadsheet is familiar to most people and it also has a limited amount of data it can store. Specifically, it is limited to just 1,048,576 rows, or 2^{20}. For those who want data with 1,048,577 entries or more, then another program will be needed. (This amount is actually an improvement for Excel spreadsheets. Back when Excel was part of Office 2007, the limit was 65,536 rows).

How does this relate to the pandemic? Well, if people in the business of collecting pandemic numbers see the number of cases growing exponentially, then they might hit software capacity limits. That happened in the UK.

The government agency that helps oversee the UK's pandemic response, Public Health England (PHE), said some 15,841 cases had been left out of national totals because of the error but did not specify what caused the so-called glitch. . . .

The 15,841 "missing" cases made public today were originally recorded between September 25th and October 2nd. All those

---

[103] The study cited in the previous footnote suggests that we could have 30 percent fewer deaths from an optimized vaccine distribution plan than something that is ad hoc.

who tested positive for Covid-19 were notified by the UK's
health authorities, but the failure to upload these cases to the
national database meant anyone who came into contact with
these individuals was not informed. It's an error that may have
helped spread the virus further [sic] through the country as
individuals exposed to the virus continued to act as normal.[104]

Why did the Excel limits matter? The UK has many more daily
cases as of this writing, around twenty-five thousand. That is well
below one million, but it is above 16,384 and . . . you can see where
this is going.

If those operating the software in the UK had noticed that
the number of cases was no longer going up in the data files, the
error might have been found quickly. One partial reason for why
the software limit was not noticed stems from the fact that one
lab was apparently sending its data in a CSV format and then the
government was converting the information for use in its own
database. Another critical piece in the puzzle was the use of the
older 2007 file format in whatever macro the UK government
was using to take the lab CSV data and merge it into its broader
database. As Jonathan Asworth, the Labor Party's shadow health
secretary said, "Why are critical databases in a national pandemic
posted on Excel spreadsheets? Why aren't they using specialist database software?"[105]

---

[104] James Vincent, "Excel Spreadsheet Error Blamed for UK's 16,000 Missing Coronavirus
Cases," (The Verge, October 5, 2020), https://www.theverge.com/2020/10/5/21502141/uk-
missing-coronavirus-cases-excel-spreadsheet-error.

[105] Whitney Tesi, "An Outdated Version of Excel Led the U.K. to Undercount Covid-19
Cases," (Slate, October 7, 2020).

Figure 5.3: From the BBC Analysis of the Excel Error

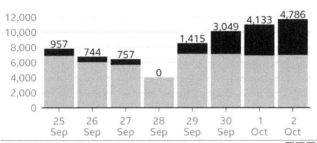

Thousands of missing coronavirus cases added after reporting problem
Number of new coronavirus cases by date reported

■ Missing cases added   ▨ Previously announced cases

Source: Gov.uk dashboard, Public Health England   BBC

How the rate of coronavirus cases changed
Positive tests per 100,000 population, week to 1 October, before and after the problem was found

Fewer than 10   10 to 24   25 to 100   100 to 199   Over 200   No data

As of 2 October   As of 4 October

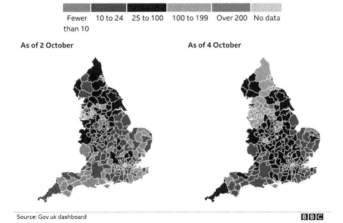

Source: Gov.uk dashboard   BBC

Was this a big error? It is hard to say, but the BBC analyzed the missing cases, and the results are in figure 5.3.[106] These are very large numbers.

---

[106] BBC, "Covid: Test Error 'Should Never Have Happened,'—Hancock," (October 5, 2020), https://www.bbc.com/news/uk-54422505.

The lesson from all this is very simple: To manage mission-critical data, we have to ensure that the management system is robust. The UK did what I suspect many governments have done, which is to cobble together pandemic data collection systems on the fly. The UK's system had to deal with labs that each had their own procedures, and then it had to stitch things together. That worked until it did not. Frankly, the mistakes seem big enough to have been policy relevant.

Could this have been avoided? It certainly seems so. An essay by D.J. Patil,[107] the former chief data scientist of the United States who spent the early days of the Covid-19 crisis working with the California government, was somewhat prophetic.

> Much of our current public health infrastructure was built to manage tuberculosis and measles and it is not up to the task of managing Covid. These outbreaks tended to be small enough to count cases in a notebook and in narrowly defined populations, impacting hundreds rather than millions of people and only a few hospitals. The evidence for the antique-ness of our public health infrastructure is the difficulty [of] obtaining timely, accurate information on the number of infections, hospitalization rates, the infected fatality ratio, and deaths. As a result, journalists and citizen-scientists have filled a gap with their own sophisticated efforts such as the The COVID Tracking Project, *The New York Times,* the *Los Angeles Times,* the *San Francisco Chronicle,* Propublica, John Hopkins University, etc.
>
> The basis of our public health reporting system is the case report. This onerous process requires significant time from both physicians and public health officials, often resulting in only partially completed forms limiting the insights that can be drawn from the data. Additionally, the data collected

---

[107] D.J Patil, "6 Lessons Learned to Get Ready for the Next Wave of Covid," (Medium, July 22, 2020), https://medium.com/@dpatil/6-lessons-learned-to-get-ready-for-the-next-wave-of-covid-ee595766d4cb.

are aggregated by public health officials before being sent to the state and CDC. The standard for a case report is that the information is comprehensive and perfect, even peer reviewable, which makes them highly useful in retrospect but also full of confidential health information which makes them hard to share. The resulting time lag and arduous reconciliation process is frustrating to both policy makers and the public.

And he offered a solid recommendation:

Given advances in the data infrastructure and cloud computing we need to *invest in a unified data infrastructure to support the reporting of Covid-19 cases from both the increasing venues where testing will be conducted (including at home tests and daily worker tests) and the traditional medical centers.* This system will need to have seamless interoperability with the electronic medical systems of the major hospital networks, support the mobile surveillance testers, and interoperable with other states' systems. Finally, we need an improved model to match data from patients as they move across regions. Afterall, Covid-19 will not adhere to state or political lines.

This encapsulates the broad need for a surveillance data strategy and infrastructure to support pandemic management.

6
Personal Risk Management

In my experience, public health experts tend to be constantly frustrated that so many people will not act on clear health advice that is in the interests of their own health. Not smoking, safe sex, weight management, and getting flu vaccines are all things that clearly lead to healthier, longer lives; and yet, many people disregard these practices. As a result, the public health experts are often scarred, exasperated, and doubtful that they can be persuasive. Thus, they often push for policies that mandate behaviors and remove individual choice.

So it was with Covid-19. Lockdowns, mandated mask wearing, social distancing, and the like were all enacted policies because public health officials did not believe people would manage their own risks. Interestingly, the evidence suggests that this time around The People largely defied those expectations. Around the world, populations have done remarkably well in following public health advice. It shows up in the data.

> The evidence on this is actually very clear. While the pandemic has its ebbs and flows, a month or so after the first significant outbreak in a region (say, a city like New York or a state like Illinois) things stabilize. The virus doesn't go away. Instead, the number of new infections is about the same from day to day. Epidemiologists refer to this situation as the reproduction

rate of the virus going to 1, with every person who is infected spreading it to just one other person on average. (Getting the reproduction rate under 1 is the beginning of the road to stopping the pandemic.)

This stands in contrast to earlier predictions of a large outbreak as the virus spread quickly at much higher reproduction rates based on how easily the virus could jump from person to person. In the absence of behavioral change, an international team of researchers predicted that an infected person would infect two to three other people. That happened right at the beginning of the pandemic, but then it changed. Part of this was due to governments instituting lockdowns but, somewhat amazingly, people locked themselves down faster than governments acted.[108]

This is reflected in a study that used phone data to track visits to 2.5 million businesses in the US from March to May 2020.[109] Because some states had lockdowns while others did not, researchers could compare adjacent counties in different states. Government lockdowns reduced visits, but 60 percent of the cases would have happened even without the lockdowns. People took care to manage their own risk.

This similar pattern happened worldwide.[110] People practiced social distancing even when no one in their personal relational networks had fallen ill. When Tom Hanks announced he had Covid-19, mobility dropped everywhere within a week. People followed the recommendations of public health officials. Why? A key part of the

---

[108] Joshua Gans, "A Hidden Success in the Covid-19 Mess: The Internet," (Stat, November 11, 2020), https://www.statnews.com/2020/11/11/a-hidden-success-in-the-covid-19-mess-the-internet.

[109] Austan Goolsbee and Chad Syverson, "Fear, Lockdown, and Diversion: Comparing Drivers of Pandemic Economic Decline 2020," *Journal of Public Economics* 193, (2020): 104311.

[110] A study of four African countries revealed that information flows increased people's adherence to mask wearing and social distancing instructions. Source: Anne E. Fitzpatrick, Sabrin A. Beg, Laura C. Derksen, et al., "Health Knowledge and Non-Pharmaceutical Interventions During the Covid-19 Pandemic in Africa," (NBER Working Paper Series, no. 28316, January 2021).

story is that, thanks to the Internet and the like, information spread quicker than the virus. Even when official guidance regarding measures like mask usage flipped, the information got out there. To be sure, it is easy to find examples of noncompliance. But the majority of people in virtually all places were compliant.[111]

This illustrates another role of information in pandemics: to help people manage their own risk. Like other aspects of pandemic management, information allows us to avoid "one size fits all" mandates. This can actually improve compliance overall and make health guidelines more efficiently applied. The question we should be asking is: What information do people need to adequately manage their own risk?

In this chapter, I will suggest two such avenues. The first is information regarding a person's exposure to others. The second is information regarding whether a person's network has infections, in which case he or she would need to adjust the level of care.

Managing the Contact Budget

As an economist, I like the idea of budgets. A good budget can tell us when something is scarce and therefore should be consumed with care. When it comes to the management of risk in a pandemic, people need a "contact budget" of how many people they have had contact with, how often, and for how long.

Basically, a contact budget is an upper limit on the number of contacts people should have during a pandemic. If people don't want to get Covid-19, they need to avoid contact with *infectious* people. That is easier said than done because we often don't know whether someone is infectious. Of course, to really play it safe a person could avoid contact with *all* people, which would, by default,

---

[111] What drove them to be compliant is still an open question.

include infectious people. Somewhere between having contact with all people and total isolation is a point where having some contact with others makes sense. But what is that point?

The basic unit of measurement for a contact budget would be a "contact minute"; that is, the number of minutes of close contact between individuals. We would also need to apply some weights related to circumstances. For instance, maybe a certain threshold of contact minutes would be required for a person to be truly at risk. Another situational variable would be whether those minutes occurred indoors, which would increase risk compared to outdoor encounters. And there is the factor of whether the individuals wear masks during the encounters.

The next question is related to the contact budget's timeframe, the period of time during which people should carefully manage contacts. We could have a daily budget, but many activities involve extensive interactions whereas other activities are more solitary. Although this is just a guess, I suspect that a weekly budget is the way to go; however, we would need to fine tune our efforts based on the properties of the virus. A monthly budget probably would not be adequate for the task. Regardless, what matters most is to have a budget. That is more important than the time allotted for it.

After addressing units and timeframe, the next question is the most critical: How much should we be allowed to "spend"? That is, how many contact minutes are reasonable over, for example, a week. Here, the budget, serving as a guide for behavior rather than as a constraint imposed by others, must reflect individual risk preferences. The right metric is likely to be related to the probability that each person has for contracting Covid-19 over, say, the next year?

This calculation requires some careful thinking. Covid-19 can be a crappy disease to get, especially for someone like me who feels old every time I look at mortality statistics as a function of age. So, let's suppose that I set my probability of catching Covid-19 at one in a hundred. How does that translate into a budget? Importantly, a 1 percent chance is not 1 percent each day; it's 1 percent over the next year or so. That is, if I want to live with a probability of greater than 99 percent that I will not contract Covid-19 over 365 days, and if the daily probability of infection for me is p, I need the following to be true:

$$0.99 < (1 - p)^{365} \text{ or } p < 0.00275\%$$

Well, that escalated quickly. As I write, the number of people in Toronto with Covid-19 is about seven thousand out of a population of three million. If I had random contact with one person on a given day, p would be about 0.233 percent, which is way over my contact budget. It is not necessarily as bad as that, because those seven thousand people with Covid-19 probably would not be out and about. So, what I would worry about is the thousand people who find out they have Covid-19 on any given day. And I would worry about another thousand or two thousand people who don't know they have Covid-19. But even in those scenarios, p is unlikely to be below 0.1 percent.

This puts things in perspective. Every visit to the grocery store might involve exhausting my entire budget.[112] Visiting other people's houses is a no-no. What about the gym or a restaurant? What if I had kids going to school? And if I had to work with others, I might not be able to mitigate my risk to acceptable levels at all. What this suggests is that underlying prevalence matters. It really makes a difference whether there are several thousand people in Toronto who potentially have Covid-19 compared to several hundred people.

Nonetheless, accounting will be at the core of being able to manage contacts. I imagine this could be usefully done if everyone had a smartphone app that used Bluetooth to count our contacts

---

[112] That said, you can manage that by trying to avoid crowds. An app called Crowdless (https://crowdlessapp.co) tells you how crowded a place is. Google Maps also has this type of functionality. This might be useful even when there isn't a global pandemic.

with other people. As we approached our contact limits, the app would remind us to "spend" less.[113]

Knowing Your Network

A contact budget is useful for managing contacts with people you don't know, but most people contract Covid-19 from people they do know. In other words, being able to manage personal risk requires knowing our own networks and how connected our networks are with other networks.

For instance, my spouse (like me) lives a hermit life except when she visits the gym twice a week. There she encounters three other people (it is a small gym). She also goes to a book club once a month and that adds another five people to the mix! These are low-risk activities (the book club gatherings occur outdoors), but they are not zero-risk.

The real problem is our kids. One is off in another city, so no problem there. Another is doing college remotely from home and the other is in high school. Remote college puts my son in the same category as my spouse in terms of contacts. The higher schooler, when school reopened, is another matter entirely.

She goes to school every other day. Prior to the pandemic, she took public transportation to school, but we decided to drive her so as to reduce exposure. Her school has four hundred students, but she is in a group of two hundred and therefore doesn't have contact with all of them. Her usual class contacts total fifteen kids, but those fifteen people meet every other day with their own networks.

How can we put all of this together? Aaron Carroll, writing in

---

[113] Some of these tools exist. A website called MicroCOVID (https://www.microcovid.org) assists you in considering a risk budget (similar to a contact budget). Source: Gregory Barber, "How Many Microcovids Would You Spend on a Burrito?" *Wired*, January 12, 2021, https://www.wired.com/story/group-house-covid-risk-points.

The New York Times, urges us to make good trade-offs lest we fall into "all or nothing" behavior.

> Each decision we make to reduce risk helps. Each time we wear a mask, we're throwing some safety on the pile. Each time we socialize outside instead of inside, we're throwing some safety on the pile. Each time we stay six feet away instead of sitting closer together, we're throwing some safety on the pile. Each time we wash our hands, eat apart and don't spend time in large gatherings of people, we're adding to the pile.
>
> If the pile gets big enough, we as a society can keep this thing in check.[114]

Carroll's point was that we should be less frustrated at the few people not doing what they should and start appreciating what people are doing.

> To keep the pile big enough, though, we need to be willing to trade some activities for others. If people want to play on a sports team, for instance, they should consider giving something up to do so. Increasing their risk by participating in a group activity should prompt them to reduce their risk the rest of the time. . . .
>
> We could choose to engage in just some of those things. We could decide to get a massage *or* get our nails done *or* have a haircut—instead of demanding that all of these and more be available to us simultaneously.

This is good advice. It is a heuristic. It is not exact, but it is a way of managing contacts even if we don't know how much we really have in our contact accounts.

That said, it is tricky. For instance, Carroll uses this logic to argue with his daughter about visits with friends.

---

[114] Aaron E. Carroll, "When It Comes to Covid-19, Most of Us Have Risk Exactly Backward," *The New York Times*, August 28, 2020, https://www.nytimes.com/2020/08/28/opinion/coronavirus-schools-tradeoffs.html.

My daughter argues that as long as she's seeing all of her friends together in school, they should be able to gather together in their houses as well. Unfortunately, she has risk exactly backward. She's not alone; lots of Americans do.

My kids, like most in Indiana, have been back at school since mid-August. Each time my ninth and eleventh grader head off to high school, they spend more time among other human beings in a day than they had cumulatively all summer. Because of that, they along with many of their friends and those friends' parents think that there's less reason to be careful in other aspects of their lives.

But as we loosen restrictions in some areas, we should be increasing restrictions in others. If kids are going to take on more risk at school, they should find ways to be even safer outside of it. Large groupings at a friend's house are not a good idea.

I am not sure that his daughter has it backwards. If a high school girl goes to school with a friend, is it riskier to see that same friend on the weekend, or is it safer to see someone else? If the girl's friend was infected on Wednesday, she would have about the same chance of being infected by that friend on Saturday—and she cannot get infected twice. But if some other person was infected on Wednesday and she sees him on Saturday, her additional risk of becoming infected is surely higher.

What is true is this: If the girl sees friends at school, she should see fewer other people during weekends. This is why going to school and then going to a weekend sports activity is likely to be worse than going to a school sports activity (without external teams).

This seems complicated but, with modern technology it is not out of the question to know enough about our networks to help us manage risk. Po-Shen Loh is a mathematics professor at Carnegie Mellon University. Recently, he showed that contact tracing apps, the ones that notify people when they have been exposed to someone with Covid-19, had it all wrong. After all, the only actions a person should take after he or she has had direct exposure is to get tested and to isolate, so as to protect others. What we really need, Loh argued, is the ability to manage our risk of exposure *before* we are exposed.

Loh put together and launched the NOVID app to do just that. It is now being used at college campuses across the US.[115] The app keeps track of a person's contacts and builds a picture of the people with whom he or she interacts closely. This is information we need and want to know. When we meet with one friend, the app shows us all the people with whom that person has had contact.[116] If someone, somewhere (who has the app) tests positive, then we get a notification of how "far away" that exposure was (degrees of separation). If a contact budget is like a calorie counter, NOVID is like a weather forecast.[117] As Loh told Cowen:

> Suddenly, the main purpose of the intervention is no longer to protect others from you (quarantining after being exposed). Instead, it is to directly protect you from others, because that early warning of approaching Covid lets you know it's a good time to wear a better mask, or to be more vigilant about distancing, because the situation is getting hot. This appeals to self-protection instincts instead of altruistic instincts. Since this app is already in deployment, we know anecdotally, for example, of a person who installed the app because his kid was going to a university that was using the app. Why? So that he could be alerted in case Covid started spreading his way from

---

[115] See: https://www.novid.org, and GeorgiaTech at https://rh.gatech.edu/news/637985/exposure-notification-app-enlists-smartphones-coronavirus-battle.

[116] S.M. Goodreau, E.D. Pollock, J.K. Birnbaum, D.T. Hamilton, M. Morris, "Can't I please just visit one friend?" (Statnet, April 3, 2020), http://statnet.org/COVID-JustOneFriend.

[117] Po-Shen Loh, "Accuracy of Bluetooth-Ultrasound Contact Tracing: Experimental Results from NOVID iOS Version 2.1 Using 5-Year-Old Phones," (NOVID, June 26, 2020), https://www.novid.org/downloads/20200626-accuracy.pdf.

the university via his kid.[118]

This gives us the opportunity to prepare by managing our contact budgets more carefully, or by pulling out that N95 mask we have been saving for a special occasion. That said, like exposure notification apps, NOVID functions best when many people have installed it.

[118] Tyler Cowen, "Novid—A Pre-Exposure Notification System for Covid (and Other Things)," (Marginal Revolution, October 30, 2020), https://marginalrevolution.com/marginalrevolution/2020/10/novid-a-pre-exposure-notification-system.html.

7

Contact Tracing

T hus far, we have focused on pandemic information solutions that involve identifying people who are infectious with Covid-19. By doing this, those people can be isolated before they infect other people thereby breaking chains of transmission. However, unless screening is literally perfect, there will always be situations in which we encounter others who are infected. If we can predict who those other people are likely to be, so that they can be isolated quickly before infecting others, we can gather helpful information and get ahead of the virus.

The primary means for predicting whether someone is likely to have been infected with Covid-19 is to investigate whether the person has been exposed to people known to carry Covid-19. This type of investigation is called "contact tracing." Its name describes what it is: a tracing procedure to identify all those who had contact with a known case.

Public health officials use various methods to carry out contact tracing. In South Korea, a digital infrastructure has been established that allows authorities to correlate the location data of any known Covid-19 case with people who crossed paths with that infected person during a period of likely infectiousness. This involves using cellphone data and also other data, such as credit card transaction locations. In some cases, CCTV cameras are used to investigate exposures and identify contacts. Suffice it to say, these measures involve a clear trade-off between solving the information problem and the strength of privacy regulations. That trade-off was something I discussed in detail in *The Pandemic Information Gap*. The bottom line is that privacy is not free. Relaxing privacy protections can allow for outbreak control.

South Korea has used a combination of testing and contract tracing to manage the Covid-19 pandemic without the need for broad lockdowns, but Japan has relied heavily on contact tracing itself without widespread testing. This has proved sufficient thus far to avoid widespread lockdowns. The Japanese have, however, also relied on milder forms of density restrictions indoors, mask wearing, and prohibitions on large crowds. Hence, the postponement of the 2020 Tokyo Olympics.

The Japanese approach was born of the challenge to control tuberculosis.

In 2018, 16,789 Japanese contracted tuberculosis and more than 2,200 died—more than double the number—892—who have succumbed to Covid-19 so far. Japan has the world's oldest population, as well as a significant influx of overseas workers, which has added up to a surprisingly major TB risk for such a prosperous nation.

Japan was an early mover in national healthcare and the current system was established in 1937. Takatorige asserts the reason Japan was able to deal more effectively with Covid-19 than Europe and the US is its hundreds of public health centers, originally designed to cope with TB.

The system's core was the Tuberculosis Prevention Association, which handled research, the development of countermeasures, and the training of public health center workers. Today, the centers are not staffed by doctors. They are administrative, rather than treatment facilities.

From this grew Japan's present public health care center-orientated approach to infectious diseases. Because hospitals are often vectors for infectious diseases, the professor notes, a key role for the 469 public health centers is as "gate guardians," determining who should be tested, thereby discouraging people from overrunning the hospitals.[119]

This infrastructure was deployed in the Covid-19 fight. One thing that aided the Japanese approach was that Covid-19 spread in an uneven way, with 80 percent of infections driven by fewer than 20 percent of infected people—the so-called "super-spreaders." This meant that outbreaks, when they occurred, arose in clusters. If a cluster could be identified and isolated quickly, it was possible to prevent broader spread of the virus.

In contrast to many recent methods that use smartphone apps to identify contacts, the Japanese approach is personnel heavy. Contract tracers are trained to go out and use person-to-person tracing at the local level to identify contacts and ensure they are isolated and tested. This "boots on the ground" approach can be very effective, unless there is a widespread outbreak. In that case, it would be difficult to scale up. This is precisely why it has been hard to replicate in countries where Covid-19 cases were already widespread. But it has been very effective at keeping outbreaks short when Covid-19 prevalence is very low.

Looking Backward

The method of contact tracing pursued in most countries is called "forward tracing." When a case is identified, contact tracers look for people who had contact with that infected person, and for those in that network who might have spread the virus too. But Japan does not rely solely on that approach. The Japanese also use

---

[119] Ake Adelstein, "Japan's Contact-Tracing Method Is Old but Gold," *Asia Times*, June 2, 2020, https://asiatimes.com/2020/06/japans-contact-tracing-method-is-old-but-gold.

another method of tracing—backward or retrospective contact tracing.

Backward tracing seems counterintuitive. After all, the "index" case who is identified as having Covid-19 is likely to have had contact with other people since becoming infected. So, getting ahead of the transmission surely involves finding those people.

But there is another effect at work: If "Jack" has been infected with Covid-19, it is likely that the person who infected him ("Jill") has infected other people too. In fact, Jill has probably infected more people than Jack. Thus, if health officials have scarce contact tracing resources, working backward to find the primary case (Jill) who infected the index case (Jack) will allow them to find more people who have been exposed and perhaps infected.

As stated above, the goal of backward tracing is to find out who infected the index person (Jack) in the first place. So, health workers need to find the contacts who interacted with Jack at the time when he was likely to have been infected. Again, having the Ct score (with multiple time points) can assist in identifying the likely time period when Jack was infected. Otherwise, it is just a guess. Mathematically, forward tracing identifies a subject's R (reproduction number) while backward tracing shows us R scaled up by a factor related to the context of how an outbreak cluster arose.[120]

This is all related to the Friendship Paradox, which is the mathematical explanation for why my friends have more friends than I do. The reason is sampling bias. If I have a friend, then it is likely that my friend has friends. And because some people out there are really popular, it's likely that there are many people who are more popular than me. Statistically, I am not likely to be the most popular person.

---

[120] Akira Endo et al., "Implication of Backward Contact Tracing in the Presence of Over-Dispersed Transmission in Covid-19 Outbreak," *medRxiv* (August 1, 2020), https://doi.org/10.1101/2020.08.01.20166595.

Now apply this to contact tracing. Suppose that a school, for example, provides frequent screening. Suppose that someone at the school tests positive. Knowing that, we can then identify the infected person's forward contacts. The total number of people we would expect to pick up via that process is related to the infected person's R number. But if that person has only had contact with others in that school, that R number will be quite low. In other words, the value of forward contact tracing is relatively low.

What about backward tracing? Here the value is enhanced. It is likely that the subject contracted the virus from someone outside of the school. That means that there is high value in identifying the source of the infection, via backward tracing.

The value of backward tracing increases dramatically if we begin to screen people in specific locations, such as schools or workplaces. If policymakers and health officials decide to invest in tools, such as apps, that make tracing easier, they need to ensure that those apps are used to trace people outside of each specific location. They should also encourage more people outside the location to use the tools. Keeping track of outside contacts is more important than keeping track of inside contacts.[121]

Contact Tracing Works

One thing social scientists know well is how hard it is to determine whether an intervention (such as contact tracing) works. We intuitively believe that contract tracing helps reduce infections by proactively identifying and isolating people exposed to a virus. But it's not that simple. Imagine that location A has pursued

---

[121] This raises the obvious issue that there are externalities present in these decisions. Organizations will have a strong incentive to keep their places managed but a much lower incentive to do so for those outside, which is precisely what backward tracing is designed to do.

contact tracing and location B has not. We discover, as expected, that location A has fewer infections than location B. Does that mean that contact tracing caused the lower number of infections in location A? That's a possibility. But it could also be that contact tracing was adopted at location A precisely because there were few infections to begin with; the low number of infections there made the tracing effort more manageable. In other words, causation may go the other way.

Here's another problem. In the interests of good "science," to discover causation, scientists sometimes choose *whether* to intervene with contact tracing and *where* to apply it. They might randomly assign contract tracing to some regions and not assign it to other regions. They often do this without (this is important) telling anyone in those regions about the assignment. What gets in the way of these choices is "ethics." Frankly, if we think contact tracing is likely to be effective at reducing infections, it is surely bad to randomly exclude some regions and, moreover, not tell people about that decision. If health professionals in an excluded region lack knowledge, it makes it hard for them to take precautions.

To get over these quandaries, science progresses as if there is some cock-up that is plausibly random and unrelated to the scientific inquiry itself. Enter the UK and that error related to the Excel spreadsheet that was described in chapter 5. Recall that fifteen thousand people who were infected with Covid-19 were not properly recorded as being infected by public health authorities. That meant that (a) no contact tracing occurred in relation to those people, and (b) no one knew about the error until after the fact. This had all the ingredients of an experiment that we would not ordinarily be "allowed" to run.

Two economists saw the opportunity presented by the UK's

error and began to work.[122] The first thing they sought to determine was whether the error's impact was distributed over enough regions to matter, and if some regions had been hit harder than others. In their paper, they found variation all over England.

Now the bad news. As it turns out, the areas where the error in the data about contacts was bigger had worse health outcomes: more cases per capita and more deaths. The authors estimate that 125,000 additional infections and fifteen hundred additional deaths were caused by the error. In all likelihood they are, if anything, understating the effects, which could be twice as large.

This tells us something important. Contact tracing is extremely valuable. But it is hard to do, difficult to organize, and expensive. And if it is to be effective, it will encroach on privacy rights. The UK experience has produced the clearest evidence to date that contract tracing works, and just how valuable it is.

Preparation for Tracing

In chapter 3, we discussed how the pre-risk (or prior) probability that someone might have Covid-19 impacts the clarity of the signal from any test or screen. The more likely that someone is infected with Covid-19, the more likely a test will provide a clearer signal of whether that person actually has Covid-19.

The CDC recognizes this. Figure 7.1 is a flow chart of the CDC's protocol for POC tests at nursing homes. Notice how it works. The first question is about symptoms and pre-risk. As was discussed in chapter 3, symptoms associated with Covid-19 do increase the likelihood that someone is infected. The second question, which seeks information about a person's relational

---

[122] Thiemo Fetzer and Thomas Graeber, "Does Contact Tracing Work? Quasi-Experimental Evidence from an Excel Error in England," (CEPR Discussion Paper no. DP15494, November 2020), https://ssrn.com/abstract=3753893.

Figure 7.1: CDC Flowchart for Testing Outcomes

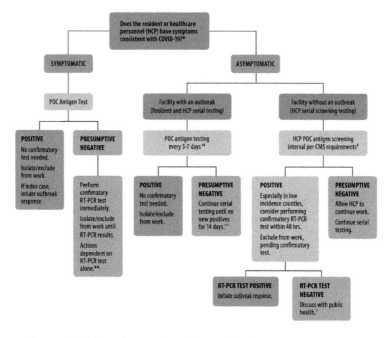

Source: CDC https://www.cdc.gov/coronavirus/2019-ncov/downloads/
hcp/nursing-home-testing-algorithm-508.pdf.

network, is also associated with risk, namely whether an outbreak might be occurring.

As the pre-risk of a person's Covid-19 infection goes up, the way the test is used changes. If a person has symptoms, the test is used for clearance purposes. In effect, symptomatic individuals are presumed to be positive (usually an unspoken fact) until tests prove otherwise. For asymptomatic people, tests are used to hopefully provide a clear signal of whether there is an outbreak. If there is no clear sign of an outbreak, health professionals remain uncertain and want more tests. I should say that a test outcome is presumptive in both cases. Public health officials don't say that, but the request for more testing in each case speaks louder than words.

The point is that pre-risk matters. If we use a rapid test with a 15 percent false negative rate and a 2 percent false positive rate, and if the pre-risk is one in four thousand, a positive test result only gives us a 1.1 percent chance of actually being positive. A negative test hardly offers us any additional information. Jump that pre-risk probability up to 5 percent and the positive test gives us a 69 percent chance of being an actual infection and a negative test result drops the risk to less than 1 percent.

But the CDC guidance, while based on pre-risk, doesn't actually offer any numbers. And the numbers matter. There are outbreaks and there are *outbreaks*. There is high and low incidence. It seems like we could do better.

In effect, we want more information than just symptoms, population prevalence, and close contact outbreaks. There would surely be a big difference between someone who just moves between home and work each day and someone who has multiple points of contact with other people. Surely, we need that information.

The irony is that we could have it. The same contact tracing apps that indicate whether an individual has had contact with an infectious person could be used to assess pre-risk—to develop a measure of how many people, in what settings, and for how long people have had contact with others. That information could be used to construct a proper estimate in relation to an individual's pre-risk. We could then use that estimate to provide a much more granular and accurate protocol than the CDC's.

And we would not need to violate privacy. Apps collect this information anyway; thus, they can inform us when Jill, who previously had contact with Jack, tests positive in the future. The information is there. All that is needed is to aggregate it differently and to then share that score to assist with testing protocol. When tests are supply-constrained, this approach would be a good way of sorting who needs a test and who does not.

8
Preparing for Covid-29

Covid-19 has gripped our attention. It has made us focus on the here and now, on the problems that we are immediately faced with. This book has followed that path. The solutions offered thus far are ones directed at our immediate crisis. But they are based, I believe, on some deeper principles. Specifically, the primary economic tool at our disposal for fighting the economic consequences of pandemics is the collection and use of information about infectious people. I believe, therefore, that our preparation for dealing with pandemics and inevitable future pandemic threats must involve building our information infrastructure and the decision-making skills to make use of it.

In *The Pandemic Information Gap*, I speculated that we would need to invest heavily in supranational institutions to deal with pandemics. From the vantage of 2020, that seemed like the only option.[123] Pandemics start somewhere and therefore we need to ensure that the right people know about a pandemic's onset as soon as it happens. And those right people must also have the

---

[123] I am far from the only one. Debora MacKenzie outlined the importance of strengthening supranational institutions in her book, *COVID-19: The Pandemic That Never Should Have Happened and How to Stop the Next One*, (Hachette: London, 2020). My colleague, Anita McGahan, expressed similar sentiments in "We need a Financial Stability Board for Health," *Financial Times*, May 14, 2020 that utilizes themes that I will also rely on in this chapter.

authority to act on that information, even if it means that the rights (say, of movement and trade) of those most immediately effected are subverted for the global good. This is always a tough call. Sovereignty is something we default to, and some proposed pandemic solutions are seen as moving us in the opposite direction. But faced with an unprecedented global negative externality, do we have a different option?

Now that we are farther down the track, I have to admit that I find myself backing away from regarding a supranational authority over other interests as a necessity; instead, I see this option as being potentially desirable. That is not much of a shift in thinking, but the reason for it is instructive. Having written this book, I believe there are ways to deal with the pandemic information problem at the national level. I say this knowing that we cannot necessarily rely on individuals to do the right thing at the right time, and knowing that we might not make the needed investments in information infrastructure quickly enough. Nonetheless, there is a practicality to my suggestions. As evidence, I want to revisit an economic tool we use to solve other information problems: the world-wide network of central banks.

Financial Contagion

There is something about the ebb and flow of the financial system that causes scientific minds to see the system as a puzzle to be solved. The system has periods of relative stability followed by a rise in optimism or buoyancy followed by pessimism and the bursting of bubbles. Sometimes this involves stocks, bonds, and the familiar turf of financial markets. At other times, similar patterns have impacted on housing, toys, and tulips. To a physicist, the economic boom followed by the seemingly inevitable bust looks like the law of gravity at work—the fabric can be stretched, but it will bounce back into place. That did not stop Isaac Newton from investing in what was later known as the South Sea bubble of 1719. For Newton, the investment resulted in a financial loss of today's equivalent of many millions of pounds. Bad investment decisions aside, Newton's interest in physics and investing was fitting, for many physics models have connections with economics. Indeed, the first Nobel laureate in economics, Ragnar Frisch, famously used wave dynamics to model business fluctuations.

To Robert May, one of the founders of mathematical epidemiology, the wake of the 2008 financial crisis reminded him of the way infectious diseases develop into outbreaks.[124]

> An increasing amount of work draws analogies with the dynamics of ecological food webs and with networks within which infectious diseases spread. For the latter analogy, one can view the dodgy financial devices as newly emerging infectious agents. Indeed, the recent rise in financial assets and the subsequent crash have rather precisely the same shape as the typical rise and fall of cases in an outbreak of measles or other infection.

He went on: "One basic question, of course, is how to prevent a problem that arises in one bank from cascading through the entire banking system. Here, insights from medical epidemiology have been helpful, and indeed the word *super-spreader* is now used often." To May, the association between epidemiology and various aspects of financial crisis was "clear."[125]

It is a stretch to consider the ups and downs of financial prices and economic activity as having a similar pattern to fluctuations in the number of cases during a pandemic. There is a boom and a bust to those cases, but generally speaking, typical pandemic paths do not mimic market patterns. However, there is an interesting

---

[124] A. Haldane and R. May, "Systemic Risk in Banking Ecosystems, *Nature* 469, (2011): 351–355, https://doi.org/10.1038/nature09659.

[125] Robert May in Paul Fine, et al., "John Snow's Legacy: Epidemiology Without Borders," *The Lancet* 381, no. 9874, (2013): 1302-1311.

linkage between epidemics and financial instability. This can be described with the concept of contagion. Optimism that leads to booms is like a contagion that can afflict even someone like Isaac Newton. Pessimism is similarly like a contagion, compelling people to suddenly change their minds about the market—sometimes like Wile E. Coyote when he has already passed the edge of a cliff. It is, therefore, tempting to think in terms of critical mass. When there are many optimistic people, those people convince others to view things the same way. When some investors turn pessimistic, it takes a while for people to realize that something is wrong and then run for the exits. We saw this play out in late 2020, with a dramatic rise (again) in the price of Bitcoin, an asset that involves such an abstract foundation that its value is often merely based on the opinions of others. This is similar to other odd bubbles in history, such as those for tulips centuries ago when single bulbs rose to prices ten times the annual income of typical workers. When *that* bubble burst, investors at least had a tulip in hand.

The links between pandemics and market fluctuations lead many economic policymakers to adopt the language of infectious diseases to explain financial instability. Consider what Andrew Haldane of the Bank of England said in 2009:

> These similarities are striking. An external event strikes. Fear grips the system which, in consequence, seizes. The resulting collateral damage is wide and deep. Yet the triggering event is, with hindsight, found to have been rather modest. The flap of a butterfly's wing in New York or Guangdong generates a hurricane for the world economy. The dynamics appear chaotic, mathematically and metaphorically.

> These similarities are no coincidence. Both events were manifestations of the behavior under stress of a complex, adaptive network. Complex because these networks were a cat's-cradle of interconnections, financial and non-financial. Adaptive because behavior in these networks was driven by interactions between optimizing, but confused, agents.

Seizures in the electricity grid, degradation of ecosystems, the spread of epidemics and the disintegration of the financial system—each is essentially a different branch of the same network family tree.[126]

Haldane was interested in the tendency of investors and others to engage in "flight" when things start to crash. They leave the system and "hide" in a manner quite similar to social distancing in a pandemic. Haldane's analogy, however, is not perfect. In the case of market crashes, when more people hide, the economic conditions grow worse, which is the opposite of what happens to health conditions during a pandemic. Despite that difference, Haldane's point is valid. When assessing the probability of instability and risk of widespread contagion, both epidemiology and finance come to the same conclusion: Global interdependence is the source of risk. Therefore, we need ways to break transmission chains so as to calm the waters. Specifically, if the problem is with some institutions that engage in risky behaviors, maybe we need to put a ring around those institutions so that we can protect "ordinary" activities. In other words, we need to reduce interdependencies.

Contagion and Information

Analogies lead people to notice not just similarities, but also differences. Mathematician and epidemiologist Adam Kucharski saw one rift:

To get infected during a disease outbreak, a person needs to be exposed to the pathogen. Financial contagion can also spread through tangible exposures, like a loan between banks or an investment in the same asset as someone else. The difference

---

[126] Speech by Andrew G. Haldane, executive director of financial stability, Bank of England, delivered at the Financial Student Association, Amsterdam, April 28, 2009, https://www.bis.org/review/r090505e.pdf.

with finance is that firms don't always need a direct exposure to fall ill.[127]

We could propose trying to isolate potentially problematic financial behaviors, but how can that be done if there is no direct relationship between the people taking excessive risks and everyone else who ends up being caught in the wake?

Simple stories of financial contagion often miss a critical ingredient: information. Unreasonable booms, and the magnitude and speed of busts, are both accompanied by an information failure.

The easiest way to see this is to consider a bank. A bank takes deposits from savers and then lends money to other people. Its job is to make sure that it assesses the creditworthiness of borrowers. That involves gathering information. Critically, this information is not shared with savers. After all, what would they do with that information? It is the bank's job to find creditworthy borrowers and to give savers a return on their savings. In ordinary times, no one wants to be the wiser.

All of this relies on whether depositors have a certain degree of confidence in the bank. They know the bank does not keep their money in a vault, and they know that the bank will give them "on-demand" access to their money should they want it. The whole exercise is a bet that things will remain ordinary. However, should depositor confidence in the bank falter, things will quickly not add up. In theory, that loss of confidence could be caused by nothing other than fear itself. In that situation, the fact that depositors do not know who the creditworthy borrowers are would become a reason for why their fears cannot easily be allayed.

Fortunately, depositors do not all wake up one day with a loss in confidence. Instead, information percolates, which causes them to reassess their beliefs regarding whether a bank can return their money. That situation has been fundamentally solved. Following

---

127 Kucharski, Adam. *The Rules of Contagion,* (New York: Basic Books, 2020), 79.

the Great Depression, banks around the world engaged in a quid pro quo with the government. In return for accepting additional regulation and oversight, which involved sharing information about their activities with the government, the government agreed to guarantee deposits. That guarantee removed the rationale for a potential loss of confidence in the banks. Thus, people could happily continue in their ignorance while the banks could do their job.

That is how we solved the issue depicted in the film *It's A Wonderful Life*. In this area, ordinary people are pretty well protected. But the financial system is itself a sly beast. It invents new ways of moving money around, from those who want to save to those who want to spend. In so doing, banks end up accepting deposits for other banks and non-bank financial institutions. In other words, the banks are now taking our deposits and mixing them with others under the same conditions of ignorance that exposed the whole system in the first place. Those pooled bank deposits are not guaranteed. Such conditions undermine confidence and leave the system exposed. This is precisely what happened in 2008 when banks suddenly realized that the mortgage-backed securities they were offering to investors were based on subprime lending (an issue of poor creditworthiness). Prior to the crash, investors had no easy way to find out the truth.

This is why the pandemic information problem draws on language (and that is no accident) from the financial information problem. A financial system crisis involves people who decide to not participate in the financial system (they hide). Depositors withdraw their funds and put them under proverbial mattresses or in some other "safe" asset. They run for safety not because they believe that all bank and financial institution activities are bad, but because they believe that *some* borrowers to whom they are lending are not creditworthy. If investors lack adequate information, they might treat *all* borrowers as being equally bad. Precisely the same type of withdrawal from social and economic activity occurs when people learn about a disease that is spreading through the population—*if* they lack information about who, specifically, is infectious. In a context of uncertainty, people will often "hide" because they don't want to risk losing everything.

To restore confidence—during market crashes and pandemics—people must be able to quickly identify the specific problems and separate them from the whole system. We have already seen the challenges associated with that in pandemics, and also how an infrastructure to produce that information is possible, but rarely available. In financial systems, that job falls mainly to central banks.

Central banks might be in the dark about some institutions, but they know a lot about others with whom they have been working and monitoring for years. In those cases, they have more information on which to base their confidence (or not). For those financial institutions that are found trustworthy, central bankers are happy to be a lender of last resort. More often than not, central banks end up making money on loans to trustworthy institutions. Thus, what looks to some like a bailout is, in fact, an investment opportunity based on long-term information gathering.[128]

We want to see this same dynamic in local pandemic management. When a pandemic is on the horizon, we need a local institution that knows the risks and that is able to step in and quickly sort out who is infectious from who is not. That will require good surveillance data at a first instance, particularly about the interconnections of individuals in their networks. We will also need information about which activities can be cheaply moved to "contact free" mode. We will need to quickly roll out screening efforts to ensure that only uninfected individuals are allowed to travel, cross borders, enter schools and workplaces, etc. Screening systems will also help to keep essential services open. In other words, there is a job to be done by *local* institutions. They should be designed and equipped to keep the economy open by assessing risk—not credit risk, but individual risk of infectiousness.

---

[128] Source: Daniel W. Drezner, *The System Worked: How the World Stopped Another Great Depression,* (Oxford, UK: Oxford University Press, 2014).

Independence

The job of central banks and prudential regulation is not to prevent financial crises per se, but rather to prevent crises from spilling into other activities. In other words, the job of central banks is containment. This role is based on one principle: independence. In normal times and during crises, central banks have had independent authority over their decisions. This includes whether to order banks and others to redress problems. Central banks have had independence in deciding how to engage in market interventions, how to control the money supply, and how to manage financial and economic stability. That independence was not baked-in from the start. It was established because the consequences of political and other interferences were all too plain (and painful) to see. Politicians are frequently subject to pressure by special interests. Those groups often want, in the financial sphere, release from regulations they perceive as unnecessary. Politicians are also subject to pressure to spend too much and tax too little. Strict constraints on spending exist at the US state level, but the US Congress benefits from softer constraints. The biggest temptation at the federal level is to print a little more money to cover deficits and hope that no one will notice. And then maybe the government can print a little bit more. And so on.

Independence is, therefore, granted to the institution that is perceived to be the long-term entity—the central bank. When a central bank conducts activities with independence, there is greater confidence that it is doing so in a transparent and nonconflicted way. There is an implied recognition that a writ of confidence can only be issued if it comes from an underlying reputation of trust.

This principle is familiar in public health settings. Indeed, to endow public health officials with independence and to empower them to manage key messaging during pandemics are regarded as best practices. These practices are based on the recognition that politicians and others may not be sufficiently resolute to deal with pandemics before they break out of control. Thus, if public health officials are *not* upsetting people by their actions to contain a potential pandemic, they are likely doing it wrong.

Unfortunately, these important roles for public health officials have been confined primarily to the realm of health policy. If Covid-19 has taught us anything, it is that pandemics are also economic problems. That being true, pandemics should be handled by addressing the information problem. Not taking that into account is the primary reason why we were unprepared for the Covid-19 pandemic. We have been playing catch-up throughout the whole crisis. We need an institution that can act independently, and that is prepared and equipped to intervene and right the ship. That preparation, in this pandemic, was not there.

There are different lines of defense against infectious diseases. The front line is early warning and being able to intervene locally to protect globally. Then, at the global level, there is a role for a supranational institution. We have those in various forms, such as the International Monetary Fund for finance, but the current institutions have proven to be too weak to prevent local problems from spilling into the global arena.

Even so, we need other lines of defense. The financial arena shows us that local crises might spread. In those situations, the backstop defense lines are local institutions. They need to be free to intervene, and they need resources to be prepared. In my view, our system of central banks is a template for building local pandemic institutions. Local pandemic authorities could become a repository of public health expertise, surveillance strategies, and economics. They would serve long-term, apolitical interests. They would significantly augment local public health authorities to resolve the information problem. There would be no more funding cuts to key services (as was done in Canada) just to satisfy short-term budgetary pressures. Instead, local pandemic authorities would sit beside the military and economic institutions as a core feature of responsible modern government.

Viruses get out of control unless dealt with quickly. The fundamental challenge is an informational one. Gather the right information and we have an arsenal for attacking pandemics. However, as has been stressed repeatedly in this book, information is not gathered for information's sake. It needs to be used to inform decisions, such as whether to isolate riskier individuals from others, or deciding which areas of the economy need to be locked down. The right information has to get to the right people or entities who make the tough calls, precisely because they are the ones with the complete informational picture that others do not have. When decisions are made blindly, costs are large and actions take too long. By contrast, preemptive information acquisition enables those with the authority to stop pandemics.

In regard to Covid-19, multiple failures in obtaining information and then applying the right information to key decisions have led to our economic and social calamity. For potential Covid-29s, we need to do better. We need to take that core lesson and ensure that we have institutions with both the information and the authority to act.

About the Author

Joshua Gans is a professor of strategic management and the Jeffrey S. Skoll Chair of Technical Innovation and Entrepreneurship at the Rotman School of Management, University of Toronto (with a cross appointment in the Department of Economics). From 2013 to 2019, he was area coordinator of strategic management. Prior to 2011, he was the foundation professor of management (information economics) at the Melbourne Business School, University of Melbourne. Prior to that he was at the University of New South Wales School of Economics. In 2011, Joshua was a visiting researcher at Microsoft Research (New England). Joshua has a PhD from Stanford University and an honors degree in economics from the University of Queensland. In 2012, Joshua was appointed as a research associate of the NBER in the Productivity, Innovation, and Entrepreneurship Program.

At Rotman, he teaches entrepreneurial strategy to MBA and commerce students. He has also co-authored (with Stephen

King, Robin Stonecash, and Martin Byford) the Australasian edition of Greg Mankiw's *Principles of Economics* (published by Cengage); *Core Economics for Managers* (Cengage); *Finishing the Job* (MUP); *Parentonomics* (MIT Press); *Information Wants to be Shared* (Harvard Business Review Press); *The Disruption Dilemma* (MIT Press); *Prediction Machines: The Simple Economics of Artificial Intelligence* (Harvard Business Review Press); *Scholarly Publishing and its Discontents;* and *Innovation + Equality* (MIT Press). Most recently he is the author of *The Pandemic Information Gap: The Brutal Economics of COVID-19* (MIT Press, 2020).

Joshua has developed specialties in the nature of technological competition and innovation, economic growth, publishing economics, industrial organization, and regulatory economics. This research has culminated in publications in the *American Economic Review,* the *Journal of Political Economy,* the *RAND Journal of Economics,* the *Journal of Economic Perspectives,* the *Journal of Public Economics,* and the *Journal of Regulatory Economics.* Joshua serves as department editor of *Management Science* and associate editor at the *Journal of Industrial Economics.* He is on the editorial boards of *Games* and *Economic Analysis and Policy.* In 2007, Joshua was awarded the Economic Society of Australia's Young Economist Award. In 2008, Joshua was elected as a Fellow of the Academy of Social Sciences, Australia. He has also written for the *Financial Times,* the *Sloan Management Review,* and more than two hundred opinion pieces published in other outlets.

Lightning Source UK Ltd.
Milton Keynes UK
UKHW041248120321
380233UK00003B/807